Chelsea Watego is a Munanjahli and South Sea Islander woman born and raised on Yuggera country. First trained as an Aboriginal health worker, she is an Indigenist health humanities scholar, prolific writer and public intellectual. When not referred to as 'Vern and Elaine's baby', she is also Kihi, Maya, Eliakim, Vernon and George's mum.

I wish to acknowledge the Aboriginal and Torres Strait Islander peoples whose hands hold this book and pay my deepest respects to you and your country as traditional owners, whose sovereignty remains unceded and who we each remain accountable to.

Another Day in the Colony

chelsea watego

UQP

First published 2021 by University of Queensland Press
PO Box 6042, St Lucia, Queensland 4067 Australia
Reprinted 2021

University of Queensland Press (UQP) acknowledges the Traditional Owners and
their custodianship of the lands on which UQP operates. We pay our respects to their
Ancestors and their descendants, who continue cultural and spiritual connections to Country.
We recognise their valuable contributions to Australian and global society.

uqp.com.au
reception@uqp.com.au

Cover design by Josh Durham
Cover photograph by Michael Cook, *Broken Dreams #3* 2010, inkjet print (edition 10),
124 × 100 cm – image courtesy of the artist and Andrew Baker Art Dealer, Brisbane
Author photograph by Chelsea Watego
Typeset in 12.5/17.5 pt Bembo Std by Post Pre-press Group, Brisbane
Printed in Australia by McPherson's Printing Group

 **Queensland Government**

The University of Queensland Press is supported by the
Queensland Government through Arts Queensland.

 Australian Government | **Australia Council for the Arts**

The University of Queensland Press is assisted by the
Australian Government through the Australia Council, its
arts funding and advisory body.

A catalogue record for this book is available from the National Library of Australia.

ISBN 978 0 7022 6316 3 (pbk)
ISBN 978 0 7022 6486 3 (epdf)
ISBN 978 0 7022 6487 0 (epub)
ISBN 978 0 7022 6488 7 (kindle)

University of Queensland Press uses papers that are natural, renewable and recyclable products made
from wood grown in well-managed forests and other controlled sources. The logging and manufacturing
processes conform to the environmental regulations of the country of origin.

MIX
Paper from responsible sources
FSC® C001695

*This book is dedicated to Vernon Thomas Watego
and Matthew Kehi-Toka Bond.*

*I am eternally grateful for the life, love and learning
that you both have gifted me.*

contents

acknowledgements

I want to acknowledge my children Kihi, Maya, Eliakim, Vernon and George, who typically experience their mum's work via absence. I want to thank you for 'family time', sunshine songs and kitchen table conversations that made us laugh, cry and think. I am so very proud of the people you are, and I'm so very sorry for the things you've had to experience; things that should never have shaped a childhood, but nonetheless did.

I want to thank my mum for always being there for me, in whatever way she could as a mother to me and grandmother to my children. I know you knew there was an incommensurability with our experiences as women and as mothers and I'm so very grateful to you for never discounting or dismissing my experiences of this world. Thank you for always being there literally, holding it down and just loving me through all of the shit.

I would like to sincerely thank Dr David Singh who helped me to think about race through my experience of it, and who over the years has guided my reading and thinking through conversations often at the drop of a hat. I feel very fortunate to call you a colleague and friend and to do the work that we get to do together. Similarly, I would like to thank Dr Bryan Mukandi who I've had the privilege to work with over many years, and who first introduced me to Paul Beatty's 'stages of

Blackness'. Bryan not only read each chapter but also reads most of my work before it goes out in the world; his cautions I don't always heed, but his time and thoughts I always value.

I must acknowledge Professor Mark Brough who has been instrumental in my academic career, starting out as an undergraduate student and research assistant, to postgraduate studies and facilitating my first academic appointment. I never understood what an academic was, nor had I ever aspired to be one; it was your generosity that defined for me what an academic could be and do, in the work, and for others.

I also want to thank my mob who have grounded me culturally and intellectually and, same time, have had my back when I needed, always bringing Black love and laughter to my life: Ali Drummond, Lisa Whop, Karla Brady, Amy McQuire, Kevin Yow Yeh, Carly Wallace, Paola Balla, Murrawah Johnson, Janet Stajic, Teila Watson and my sister Simone Watego, thank you for all that you do, including what you do for me, in just getting it. In addition I'm a beneficiary of being part of a most generous, caring and clever intellectual community so I wish to thank my friends Helena Kajlich, Alissa Macoun, Liz Strakosch, Debbie Kilroy and Anna Carlson for being there in so many ways for me and for mob.

Finally, I would like to thank Uncle Shane Coghill and Aunty/Dr Lilla Watson for mentoring and modelling the kind of Indigenous intellectual sovereignty I can only aspire to. Uncle Shane is a Goenpul Yuggera man and an 'Original Inala Boy' who has cared for me and our family in ways that I can't properly do justice to here. Uncle Shane did not teach me about sovereignty as a theory, but as something embodied, every day and everywhere. I am most grateful for the strength he has given me, particularly when I felt at my weakest. As it happens, it would be those times that Uncle Shane would always appear. I feel like he has been that boxing coach in the corner of the ring, always in the ear of his beleaguered fighter between each round, saying all the things needed for that fighter to jump up when the bell rings despite the pain and doubt felt in that body. With Uncle Shane in my corner, getting up felt less of an act, and more of a determined and deliberate form of action. Thank you, Uncle, for insisting I remember my strength as Yugambeh, never losing sight of what it is to be sovereign and never underestimating the power that matriarchal mob hold, as we stand in relationship with each other and the surrounding peoples of South East Queensland.

Aunty/Dr Lilla Watson is a Birri Gubba and Gungalu scholar who I first met as a young student at a UQ graduation ceremony while she was serving as a member of Senate. I didn't know her at the time, but she encountered me among a sea of whiteness and told me she was proud of me. I remember her handing me a hanky of hers to wipe my tears and to this day I am most fortunate to have the opportunity to sit at her kitchen table these decades later, to listen, to learn, to laugh and, still, to cry (even though she gammin tells me not to!). Aunty Lilla was very much a part of the thinking in this book and those yarns at her kitchen table, much like the ones I grew up having with my father, have shaped how I think of myself and my place, not just in the colony, but on my country.

There's a particular conversation I had with Aunty Lilla that didn't find its way into any of the chapters, but profoundly shifted the terms of reference of this book. It was the day after the thirtieth anniversary of the handing down of the report from the Royal Commission into Aboriginal Deaths in Custody. I had travelled to Sydney at the invitation of sister Gwenda Stanley to participate in a panel conversation with family members who had lost loved ones in custody. It was a day that felt more violent than most days in the colony, having heard these accounts firsthand, and in such detail. I was left feeling numb and broken. The following morning, I flew home and landed at Aunty Lilla's kitchen table, with the draft manuscript of this book. It was in this state that I was gifted with her most generous critique, one that revealed the limitations of my frame of reference but, in what it offered, healed the very despair I had been grappling with.

This book initially was one that strategised 'survival' but, having read the manuscript, Aunty Lilla looked me in the eyes and said, 'Chelsea, we are not survivors. We are more than that.' Consequently, I reconfigured my thinking to be less about surviving, and to instead centre upon our living. Similarly, Aunty Lilla called into question my reliance upon resistance. Resistance, she felt, betrayed the groundedness of Indigenous sovereignty. 'We haven't moved,' she said. 'We are holding our ground and they just keep battering us, but we are standing strong.' So in lieu of resistance, I have talked about Indigenous presence as one of insistence and persistence. You see when our sovereignty is framed as resistance, as agitation, as aggression, it is as though we are the antagonists. But we are not. And the violence we encounter for having held our ground is not of our making. We must remember that.

The final terms we talked about were 'settlers' and 'settler colonialism', which appeared to Aunty Lilla to minimise the violence of this particular form of colonialism – there is little 'settling' about a relationship in which the colonisers never leave. So, I speak instead of colonisers and, at Aunty Lilla's suggestion, colonial settlerism. I am compelled to tell of this encounter to honour and acknowledge Aunty Lilla's intellectual work, for it is hers, not mine. In doing so I also want to show how insightful, how generous, and how important the critique of Aboriginal women is in this place.

Both Aunty Lilla and Uncle Shane generously read every page of this book and entered into conversation with me with great care. I am forever thankful for the time they have taken to armour me culturally and intellectually to stand my ground, insisting that I never forget the terms on which we should be operating – ours.

foreword

This book is the truth-telling of a lone runner. Chelsea is running a race and can't see anyone in front of her and she can't see anyone behind her but she never stops running. She is not in the race to win and she is not in the race to lose either. She is in the race to tell her story, of self, which is the story of many of her mob.

She knows this story so well because she has lived it her whole life and at times it must be like a living nightmare, where you can't wake up. But it is the 'blue-sky day' that helps you (universal), keeps you sane, keeps you from falling into the pit of the colonial mentality to become one of the 'walking dead' (people who don't think). This writer knows white Australians so much better than they know themselves because, consciously or unconsciously, white Australians through acts of racism are so willing to expose to Aboriginal people the very worst parts of their nature.

So it will be a difficult book for some people to read and comprehend, or not. However, it can also be a book for readers to join a race they were not aware they were in, so they too can experience 'blue-sky days' in overcoming the burden of racism. This book is a must-read for all citizens of this country called 'Australia'.

– Dr Lilla Watson

Dr Lilla Watson is a Gungalu and Birri Gubba (Wiri) woman who has dedicated her career to the education of others, both on national and international platforms, and is co-founder of The BlackCard Pty Ltd. Dr Watson holds a Bachelor of Arts and has lectured at several universities, including the University of Queensland. She was instrumental in the development of the renowned LinkUp agency, tasked with the responsibility of reuniting Stolen Generation Children. She has been an advocate and supporter for the Aboriginal Tent Embassy, Tribal Council and several Murri youth programs. Dr Watson has also provided dedicated support to Woodford Prison, teaching and counselling Murri prisoners, as well as serving as a member of the Parole Board for Corrective Services. She has also devoted her time to serving on other boards including: the Queensland Art Gallery, the Senate of the University of Queensland and the Board of the State Library.

introduction

Every day I achieve something because I was born in this skin,
every day I concede something because I was born in this skin

Vernon Ah Kee[1]

This book was written in the year that was 2020. Best remembered for COVID-19 and a renewed global Black Lives Matter movement after the murder of African-American man George Floyd at the hands of a Minneapolis police officer. The year 2020 was also the 250th anniversary of Captain Cook's voyage along the east coast of so-called Australia. It was to be commemorated with a lavish year-long party courtesy of a $50 million tab covered by the federal government, which included sailing a replica of Cook's *Endeavour* around the continent in some sort of sordid victory lap, which Cook never actually sailed.[2] This proposed exercise was first proclaimed as a 're-enactment' of Cook's voyage and a chance for all to 'rediscover' Cook who 'gets a bit of a bad show', according to then Prime Minister Scott Morrison.[3] This expensive re-imagining of white feats and false discoveries was a reminder not just of a colonial past but a colonial present.

As fate would have it, the ship never set sail. Due to the pandemic, the ship never reached its scheduled thirty-nine locations, which included Bedanug or, as they refer to it, 'Possession Island', where Captain Cook is alleged to have 'claimed' Australia for the British Crown.[4] In lieu of the party, we were greeted with a grotesque form of eulogising of Cook which, as it turned out, included some Indigenous male commentators who testified to seeing themselves in him. We were reminded that every damn day really is just another day in the colony.

I tell of this time because this book was written in a moment.

It was a moment when my body insisted I stop. And stop I did. I took leave from work, including much of the work that I loved doing, from Twitter to Inala Wangarra to the *Wild Black Women* radio show. This moment would come to last a few months and coincided with the progression of two race discrimination cases. This was a time when I had been most productive intellectually but a time when physically my body was refusing to turn up. My body was tired and, in this moment, it appeared to insist that I tell a story, one which the bruises that had been inflicted upon it just couldn't speak to. It was here that I came to fully appreciate the importance of writing in these precise moments. And, while these moments do pass, I was reminded not to underestimate the significance of the stories told in them.

This is a book of stories, stories that are mine.

I tell these not to centre myself or to universalise my experience. I tell this story of the colony through my experience of it, as a means of adhering to an ethics of practice grounded in an Indigenous terms of reference in which knowledge is embodied and relational. In telling my stories to tell a story of the colony, I am not claiming the position of 'knower', rather I am showing how I came to know, which in turn reveals both the strengths and limitations of this work. This for me has more to do with a politics of transparency and accountability around knowledge production as a kind of showing one's working, rather than trying to be 'the one'.

I also draw upon my own stories as I am keenly aware of the extractive nature of this place, even in the genre of Indigenous writing, both fictional and factual. We are at a time in which Aboriginal authors who have discovered their ancestry are outweighing the number of authors who have grown up Aboriginal – even in accounts of growing up Aboriginal. Conversely, there is an increasing volume of Indigenous scholarship that involves the extraction of Indigenous experience in order to become the ultimate knower of it. All of these examples exact a violence on Black people, Black communities and Black consciousness, because they are a colonising practice, of discovery, and of claiming something that doesn't belong to you – yet, or at all.

Inasmuch as this book was told at a time, it is told from a place.

In telling stories from the place I come from (geographically, culturally, economically and politically), I am not claiming to know race or culture better than anyone else. I tell these stories to enter into a conversation, one which others can be privy to; one that many of us have had at our kitchen tables but not openly in public. This book is a think-out-loud story comprising a compilation of essays that seeks to engage mob in a conversation centred around strategies for living in the colony. I enter the conversation with my embodied knowledge as a Munanjahli and South Sea Islander woman who grew up in the outer suburbs of Brisbane, Queensland. I wrote this book in anticipation of the potential conversations and debates that will emerge between Blackfullas rather than the number of times the text is cited by whitefullas.

We simply don't need more texts that teach whitefullas about us on their terms. We don't need stories that muse over our humanity or authenticity as Blackfullas for them to debate. We need stories that are written by us *and* for us, that challenge us and nourish us – exclusively. Stories are powerful things, but Black stories are best of all. Black stories are not stories of Black subjects, neither are they stories told by Black people; they are stories told *by* Black people *to* and *for* Black people exclusively. Black stories are stories that don't require attending to a white audience, apologising for the presence of the white villain or punchline, or translating terms when there is clearly no frame of reference for understanding anyway.

They are those stories that make you both feel and think something about the world; they are the stories told among children out the back playing 44 home, the stories adults share sitting around the kitchen table or standing at the grave site, the ones shared through tears when drunk at three in the morning when everyone else has long fallen asleep, those stories conjured up from a song, or a photo, and the ones too funny to tell without snorting, slapping a knee or slapping someone else. Black stories are beautiful things and can be found everywhere – except on bookshelves. Koori-Rep[5] said it best when he said, 'my music's getting played without a radio station'. The demand of the market has kept too many Black stories off bookshelves, because the success of the Black story is still measured via white readership.

Yet Black stories are still told.

I love listening to stories for what they do in the telling and the teaching. Maybe it's a hangover from my Sunday school days. I hated worship time, but I loved learning through parables which were much like the creation stories that were told and/ or denied to some of us. Story as method is one that has served us well. I remember Dr/Aunty Lilla Watson speaking of the usefulness of story for oral cultures as the vehicle for retaining all the information necessary for sustaining one generation to the next. As such those stories must be repeated over and over again, so that we never forget the lessons they contain.

The stories I tell here are not necessarily 'new' stories; they are stories that I have told in part before, some as short-form op-eds, or as parts of lectures or public-speaking engagements, or as asides and anecdotes with mob. I had to get over my ill-ease at retelling them as I remembered rolling my eyes at the repertoire of stories I would hear Dad roll out with visiting family members about Uncle this, and that time cousin so-and-so did that.

I tell stories here to think not about solutions but rather strategies – strategies of coping and for combat in the colony, which might be of use to my children and theirs long after I am gone. This book is an opportunity for a kind of overhearing at the kitchen table, lessening the burden upon our children to remember when we are no longer here to tell them. I know that the challenges laying ahead for them in the colony are far greater than what came behind in maintaining that claim of 'still here'. The creative and intellectual work of Blackfullas should be dedicated to minimising the burden upon the generations to follow, or at least holding the line. As such, I love being a Black writer and a Black academic. I don't see the prefix of Aboriginal, Indigenous, Black or Munanjahli as derogatory or diminishing. The prefix makes clear not only who I am, but who I am here for, who I write for, who I labour for, all of which makes clear the standard of excellence to which I must adhere. The Black writer and scholar is not a diversity hire or disadvantage project – we are sovereign subjects who are meant to be of service to our people. What else could be more important in this place?

Another Day in the Colony is a hashtag I and other Blackfullas have used on Twitter to describe the types of colonial violence that Blackfullas are subjected to every day and everywhere in this place in real time. When I speak of violence I speak not just of the physical kind, but the emotional, spiritual, economic, intellectual and cultural kind – the conditions that enable and ensure we, as a people, are the most incarcerated, most uneducated, most diseased, most impoverished and most likely to end our own lives.

However, this is not a book about Black problems or the problem of Black people.

To speak of state-sanctioned colonial violence is not to reproduce or reinforce colonial narratives of Aboriginality as 'a' or 'the' problem, though I am conscious of the dangers of hypervisibility in our state of despair. This is a book that takes up the ideological position articulated so powerfully on Australian television in 2014 by Aunty Rosalie Kunoth-Monks when she declared, 'I am not *the* problem.'[6]

I appreciate that there is a literary market for fictions of Black problems, but this is not a book for colonisers, or those aspiring to share the same status as them. This is a book that is written specifically for Blackfullas, and when I say Blackfullas I mean of the capital B kind.

When I speak of the uppercase Blacks, I speak of those who simultaneously recognise and refuse the racialised location we've been prescribed, as well as those who have been haunted by it. In writing for/to them, I have presumed a prior knowledge and a shared frame of reference, so much so that I have refused to provide copious footnotes for others to keep up or keep a check on things. Parts of this book speak to a pain and a vulnerability that need not be fully paraded about this place, but which the Black reader no doubt will know and feel intimately.

Of course, the colonisers may find something of use here, though I find they are most comfortable with learning about us rather than from us. I have seen the sense of indignity in the eyes of whitefullas when it is suggested to them that they could learn something from the oldest living continuing culture on the planet – you know the same one they violently try to eradicate. You see when it comes to doing the educative work with the colonisers, it is not a matter of footnotes, explainers, manuals, guides or documentaries. They've already written the account of us and, regardless of how articulate we are, will always measure our account against theirs, and will always find it lacking.

I have described elsewhere my positioning as an Aboriginal academic, having watched the unease of colleagues and students as they grapple with the idea that I could exist authentically as knower and 'native' at any one time.[7] And I spoke of the advice from a most senior Indigenous scholar who stated, 'when you realise that you will never earn their acceptance, you will be free'. Freeing it is, to no longer appeal to be seen by the very people whose existence in this place is predicated upon your non-existence, as human and/or knowing. And disappointing it will be for those who know how to relate to us only through a role of servitude.

Over the years, I have become disillusioned by the prospect that my best emotional and intellectual labour was being exhausted at work, which despite being situated in 'Indigenous-specific' units of one kind or another was largely centred around catering to the colonisers, whether they were staff or students. We were to hold their hands, to be their personal tour guides into the Aboriginal prison of dysfunction they had constructed in their consciousness and were intent on maintaining. We were to overlook the daily indignities and overtly racial onslaughts, to help them 'get it', which they never really did. I remember countless times being undermined by other Blackfullas in and around those spaces because they were more preoccupied with how we looked in front of white people, rather than wanting to confront the violence that white people were enacting.

The lie we are told is that as Blackfullas we need them because there is not enough of us, so therefore we must convince them of our humanness, and teach them about 'our culture' so that maybe they will care and/or convince others of our humanity. As a strategy, this has failed us, and has meant that we relegate our needs and aspirations as a people to the very bottom, the same place we occupy on the racial hierarchy. It means we remain enslaved in domestic service to those damn colonisers.

In attending to the needs of Blackfullas, I am speaking of our literary needs. I'm speaking of the texts that must find their way into the hands and bookshelves of Blackfullas – those texts that are bought and borrowed, dog-eared, stained and worn because their words were returned to, required and rendered most useful in the living – Black living to be exact. They are not the texts that appear as pristine artefacts on display, those quaint, exotic, ancient representations of a supposed former self that also reside on coloniser bookshelves in lieu of the Aboriginal skull that once resided there.

Black writing must be of and for Black living – a living that exists beyond that of problems and solutions, and most certainly beyond hope.

But this is not a story of defeat.

Another Day in the Colony is not a resignation to the inevitability of colonial settlerism. It is a reminder of the significance of the everydayness of our existence as a people, on our terms. As a book and a hashtag, it reminds the Black reader of our strength as unwavering and of our sovereignty as unceded, despite the unrelenting violence visited upon those of us who insist on standing our ground, holding that frontline on a frontier war that is never-ending.

1

don't feed the natives

Colonialism obviously throws all the elements of native society into confusion. The dominant group arrives with its values and imposes them with such violence that the very life of the colonized can manifest itself only defensively, in a more or less clandestine way. Under these conditions, colonial domination distorts the very relations that the colonized maintains with his own culture.

Frantz Fanon[1]

So I grew up in the 1980s in one of the outermost southern suburbs of Brisbane. I remember trampolines, thunderstorms, the sound of Mr Whippy vans in summer, and the smell of kerosene heaters in winter. I remember VHS and cassette tapes and broken TV aerials, holidays that were effectively road trips to visit family for weddings, funerals and birthdays. I remember the Joh days, or at least the talk of it in our home, the days of police brutality and corruption, not to mention Joh's ban on the right to assemble, which appeared particularly egregious, at least according to the register of my father's voice. Not that my family was politically active; my dad was a truck driver and he worked, a lot. As workers, he would insist that we be members of the union, despite him never being afforded any actual protection as a Black subbie on the receiving end of a daily kind of racial violence over the years.

I remember things always being tight and tough, yet strangely safe and certain. We lived in the same home all of our lives with Mum and Dad married until death did them part. It was a union that fell slightly short of forty years, owing to Dad dying of untreatable lung cancer. Their union, that of a Black man and white woman, was remarkable as it was the first time on either side of their families in which there had been a marriage between Black and white. I remember the stories they would tell, of disapproving family members, of Mum being the one to negotiate with real estate agents to secure a home, of Dad's car being turned inside out by police while transporting my mum from work at night through the city via West End. I remember them recalling the officer's words to my white mother, 'Do your parents know you are with him?'

doesn't assimilate into other cultures very well[2]

The products of this relationship, us kids, were placed in what some might see as an in-between place – never white and nowhere near as Black as our father. This position was not so much like the veil that WEB Du Bois[3] the great African-American scholar and intellectual spoke of, but a clear line that our bodies in their being had transgressed; like that of Boundary Street in West End that my parents transgressed each night. Boundary Street was once the boundary that marked the city limit within which Aboriginal people were excluded after dark and on Sundays entirely. This boundary was a very real signifier of the marginal status that had been assigned Aboriginal people in the colony. It was more than just a street name, and the police would crack stockwhips along the perimeter to keep Aboriginal people out. Long after the law waned, they continued to police this boundary. Boundary Street represents a location in which my body is situated, the parameters defined in such a way that my body could never be located within them. It is not a borderline, being-on-the-margins kind of place; it is a supposed belonging-to-nowhere kind of place. But I want to speak of my body in terms of location because despite not meeting the criteria by which they deem it capable of existing, it exists precisely through its relationship to place. Perhaps I insist on speaking of the location of my body because it can no longer contend with those colonial assertions that it has lost its way.

I remember occupying multiple supposed in-between spaces growing up, so much so that it didn't register as discomfort or displacement. We lived across from the foundry, a train station and four lanes of traffic, which reminded us of how distant we were from the city that long excluded Black presence; even though we were not far from the boundaries of my father's traditional country as a Yugambeh man. Despite the proximity, we were not on it, much like we weren't in the city of Brisbane despite occupying the same postcode prefix. There was this strange sense of being rendered out of place, in a place that we had always been in, and from.

We were not poor in an absolute sense but we lived with an everyday urgency around not wasting things out of economic necessity. Both of my parents worked hard, their earnings not matching their outputs. Our house didn't look like other people's houses did with its mismatched mostly second-hand furniture. We were not living among our Black family and cousins who were situated to the south in Tweed Heads and to the north in Bowen, and while our white family lived in closer proximity, they never stayed in our home like our Black family members would over the years.

I remember those moments when I discovered that I was simultaneously an Aborigine but also never a real one. It truly is something, to experience something only to discover that you don't meet the criteria for how such a thing has become known – particularly by those who claim authority despite never being in relationship with that which they claim to know. It is something to discover that you belong to a category that you never knew had a name, let alone a social meaning divorced from your experience of it. To forever be evading those categorical definitions is disorienting, dispossessing even. Perhaps.

I remember the moment that I discovered I was poor, and that such a label meant that there was something lacking morally within our family home. The irony here was that if there was one thing certain in our childhood, it was the strong moral compass of my father which centred upon us being better people, rather than wealthier ones. I also remember other people (and by other people, I mean non-Aboriginal people) discovering my Aboriginal ancestry only to insist to me it was lacking culturally. It struck me, I think, because at our kitchen table, Blackness and low socioeconomic status were never talked about in terms of a product of our lack. We were to be proud of our working-poor status; it was in my father's eyes, where the real work was done. Similarly, our Blackness was not a source of shame but a source of pride because of our strength even amid struggle. It was not like we were told this as reassurance in times of crisis, when our identity came into question; it was the terms of reference from which we operated in our home.

Throughout my life I experienced these disjunctures between how I had come to know myself with those who claimed authority to know, but this disjuncture was not an experience of a different account of things; it was an embodiment of difference, or unbelonging, assigned to my body which it every day refused to accept. Some call this 'walking in two worlds'. But there is only one world that the Black body must occupy – ours.

Du Bois speaks to Black souls, in what he deemed 'double-consciousness'.[4] In his seminal text, *The Souls of Black Folk*, he describes the situation of the African American whereby 'one ever feels his two-ness, two souls, two thoughts, two unreconciled strivings, two warring ideals in one dark body, whose dogged strength alone keeps it from being torn asunder'. Du Bois says double-consciousness is 'the sense of always looking at one's self through the eyes of others, of measuring one's soul by the tape of a world that looks on in amused contempt and pity'. According to Du Bois, Black folk have the gift of second sight, yet as a result 'never have a true self-consciousness', only ever seeing 'oneself through the revelation of the other world'. Perhaps.

not a willing participant[5]

I remember doing an assignment in primary school about some foreign country. The only resource available to us at the time was the outdated second-hand 1979 edition of *The World Book Encyclopaedia* that gathered dust on our lounge-room bookshelf. The books were always at the bottom, as most shelves were stockpiled with sporting trophies and medals which were routinely dusted by the children who owned them, as part of a ritualistic stocktake of who was the most sporty. For the record, it was me. But back to the reference text for every single assignment submitted by the Watego children during their schooling years.

The other place of knowledge was the local newsagency with its trundle of school-project glossy foldout cards. Each glossy foldout card could take me to China, France, Ancient Greece and even Aboriginal Australia. The geographical location of Aboriginal Australia wasn't always clear; the land was red and dusty, the people much darker like my dad, though, unlike him, they were naked. Aboriginal Australia painted in caves and weaved baskets. This was Aboriginal Australia, I was told. This representation of Aboriginal Australia looked nothing like where or how we lived. In its knowing, it was located in another unknown time and place but, yet, it was familiar.

This account aligned with the occasional reference to us in the classroom throughout my primary school years, which my body was never situated within. This was a time in schooling life when there was no 'Black cladding' of any sort; no acknowledgement of country at assembly, no Aboriginal mural on the toilet block walls or Aboriginal and Torres Strait Islander flags at the entrance. There were no Aboriginal teacher aides; in fact, I don't remember there being any other Aboriginal families in our primary school. This was a time when the school sporting houses were named after the so-called explorers Logan, Oxley and Cunningham.

As it happens, I would go on to be captain of the Logan House. The city of Logan, which encompasses my traditional country, is named after Captain Patrick Logan, the third commandant of Moreton Bay Penal Settlement that would later become the city of Brisbane. Logan died in 1830, apparently having met his death at the hands of 'natives' – so maybe it was fitting I would lead that house after all.

I remember shifting into my secondary schooling in the early 1990s, at a time of ATSIC, Cathy Freeman carrying the Aboriginal flag (for the first time), Yothu Yindi's 'Treaty' being played on *Rage* on Saturday mornings, and a fierce brand of Indigenous leadership that would occasionally grace our screens on the nightly news. Aborigines were musical, political, angry and, man, could they run fast – with pride.

It was at this time I experienced the emergence of Aboriginal people in the curriculum in which we existed, as past and present, post 1788. One elective class I took, citizenship education, had a section on missions and reserves and the removal of Aboriginal children into dormitories. We had teaching staff dedicated to

Aboriginal programming, though aside from putting on an occasional lunch in a classroom with other kids who too were Aboriginal, they typically did not know what to do with us.

There was safety in knowing the few other Indigenous families at the school even though we were still fewer in number than the Māori and Pacific Islander and non-white families. We were suddenly less ethnically othered, but also seen as less ethnic because we didn't appear as 'the Aborigines' that they believed they knew or exotic as they expected their ethnics to be.

This was a time when my difference as Aboriginal became noticeable to others, or perhaps less marginal. People remarked on my father in his being 'Black-Black'; friends noticed the aunties, uncles, cousins who occupied the lounge room floor and who seemed to be too many in number to be actual relations.

I remember in high school encountering a dual visibility and erasure, that so many Blackfullas experience in the colony, of: 'How much percent?' 'But you're not full' 'You're not a real one.' Having never thought to question the legitimacy of the colonisers' location, it was odd to me that they would constantly question mine. I had always wondered about the function of these interrogations that were inscribed upon my body, claiming to know it better than I did. My identity was fraudulent, they insisted.

One kid was certain I wasn't really Aboriginal because I didn't eat witchetty grubs. I guess he had a point – I'm sure I read somewhere that the Aborigine eats witchetty grubs. I remember that time when I got to be 'one of those people' and it didn't require me to revert to the traditional diet of my people. It was in my senior years at a time where I was no longer a high-achieving student both in sports and scholarship. I wagged school, went to parties, got into fights and became uninterested in school life. To this day I don't recall exactly why. Others were quick to offer an explanation: it must be because 'she is one of those people'.

This was to be a fairly short-lived period of teenage rebellion in the scheme of my life, and after this time non-Aboriginal Australia returned to the task of insisting that I wasn't really Aboriginal, which was confusing because I sure as hell felt as though I was treated as one. Through these encounters I discovered what it means to them for me to be one: if the Aborigine doesn't eat witchetty grubs, they must drink alcohol or, better still, sniff petrol, something I was later accused of in the online comments of an academic editorial I had authored. Not that it bothered me all those years later; little did that anonymous knower know that at sixteen years of age I had already learnt how this discourse of deviance worked. I knew it could both authenticate my urban olive-skinned self as one of those Aboriginal Australians I had read so much about, while also operating as a device for discrediting any attempt I would make to author an account of us.

Du Bois laments, 'How does it feel to be a problem? I answer seldom a word. And yet being a problem is a strange experience.'[6]

aboriginal all the time[7]

There was a time when I thought fixing the problem of being the problem was to counter such claims with testimonies of strength and capability. I thought that we could be freed from being the problem, not simply by wresting from them the narration of the accounts, but by bringing an evidence base to the testimony.

I literally undertook a PhD attending to the problem of being a problem.[8] The problem with my approach was that I acted through a lens of identity rather than race. And the problem with identity is that the concept itself is typically one that they've set the parameters for, in terms of the 'all-knowing western self'. So much of our labour has been exhausted on testifying to our identities as though there is something actually wrong with and incomplete about them, as though the colonisers just don't *know* about us. But they do, precisely because they have made the rules that mean they are the only ones who can ever know, and they can rearrange those boundaries whenever they like and police them even when the signposts are no longer there, even when we mistakenly subscribe to the idea that our being could be articulated via an individualised articulation of an identity that is of our own choosing, just like theirs.

I can't tell you the number of Blackfullas I've encountered who at one point in their life have felt in their body, in their bones, in their heart, so deep in their soul that they weren't Black, Aboriginal, or sufficiently entitled to claim the bloodline that runs through their veins. And I am not talking here about those who have discovered their ancestry later in life: I speak of bodies birthed Black, whose knowledge of themselves ran seamlessly through generations over 60,000 years back to the land within which they first became known as human. I used to wonder how it could be that these same souls would come to question their own body, their knowing of it, and its belonging to this place.

Once we were massacred, now we are researched – known, only ever to be erased.

I remember several years ago when my daughter brought home a drawing. She was in Year 2 and had been asked to draw a picture of her culture at school for Harmony Day. Harmony Day is the colony's way of commemorating the International Day of Eliminating Racial Discrimination. In the colony, children are indoctrinated early to speak of culture rather than race. My daughter, as part of her schooling, thus drew a picture of her culture as an Aboriginal girl. She drew me in a red frock standing outside my gunya holding a boomerang, with her father above holding his spears. We were placed in our natural habitat among animals and elements that she and her four siblings are named after in Yugambeh language: Kargaru, Murun, Bilinba, Gibam and Yalgan. She had never seen her family in this setting before, but this was, according to her, at age seven, her culture. Her cultural representation placed us in another time and place, one which was unfamiliar. Or was it?

Juxtaposed with this image is the Aboriginal cultural tale of *Jedda*, the 1955 Charles Chauvel film that chronicled how 'the magic of the native mating call was stronger than the habits of civilisation'.[9] Jedda was the first colour feature film in Australia featuring 'the coloured folk'; a Blackfulla Shakespeare, if you will, centred around the forbidden love of Jedda and Marbuck. Jedda is raised in the home of the white station owner after her Aboriginal mother dies in childbirth. Despite being taught European ways, as Jedda grows up she longs for her people, and is attracted to Marbuck, referred to as 'the full-blood Aborigine'. Spoiler alert: it doesn't end well, with Jedda and Marbuck running away together only to commit suicide, having been sung a fatal death song by Marbuck's people – such is the futility of Black love, we are led to believe. The poster for the movie shows Jedda 'the uncivilised' in her red frock in her natural habitat with her love interest standing above her with his spear.

My daughter has never seen the movie Jedda or the poster, but she has been raised by two Aboriginal parents in a close-knit Indigenous community to which she *belongs*. She has been exposed to some fairly sophisticated conversations about identity, race and culture at her kitchen table each night owing to the political, cultural and intellectual work of her parents. And despite me making sure she had more than a world book encyclopaedia and glossy project card to refer to in knowing herself, when it came to articulating her culture, this was what she drew. I remember my eldest child expressing his surprise, and he asked her why didn't she draw me 'holding an award or something?' I too wondered how she had cast me in the role of Jedda, from a film that I routinely used to critique for its colonial representations of Aboriginality in the Aboriginal studies major I taught.

I tell this story not to reveal an apparent identity crisis in my seven-year-old daughter, because it doesn't show that. What is telling about this story is how my daughter knew, at such a young age, when the coloniser asked her cultural story that this was the only permissible one to tell. It speaks little to her culture as lived by her and tells more about the functionality of culture in the colonial situation. It tells a story of the ongoing violence working upon the souls of Blackfullas, men, women and children via a discourse of culture – one that is never 'living' but is always lost or less-than. It tells a story of the dispossessing function of culture, much like identity, in which we can no longer see ourselves in this place, both here and now, because of how they have defined it for us. The function of this story, much like most stories told about us, some of which are even told by us, is to serve the coloniser rather than nourish 'the native'.

In returning to *Jedda*, the audience is comforted by the narrator at the end of the film. He assures the viewer that Jedda's spirit has joined 'the greater mother of the world, in the dreaming time of tomorrow'. Even the fictional Jedda exists most comfortably in the coloniser's imagining in another time and place as deceased.

It is hardly surprising that research conducted in the 1990s by the Council for Aboriginal Reconciliation[10] examining the attitudes of non-Indigenous Australians found that 'no matter where the research was conducted, the "real" indigenous [*sic*] people were always somewhere else'. According to the colonisers, there are few real Aborigines remaining in Australia and they are really hard to find. We see in contemporary discourse about Aboriginal people every day and everywhere, how the aspiration of a dying, doomed and vanishing race is upheld.

The colonisers have long been comforted by their claims of the passing Aborigine and you can find any number of Aboriginal people who have ancestors that were once wistfully described as 'the last of their tribe'. Tasmania remains etched in the nation's collective memory as the place that 'wiped out' the Aborigine (which it didn't, by the way) and is demonstrative of their attachment to the notion of Terra Nullius – a false claim which the colonisers are still trying to make true. It is a claim that Black bodies in their presence disrupt every damn day in the colony.

I still remember my child coming home from a high-school history lesson trying to process the disruption their body presented. In that class they were discussing the Mabo decision, but not as a matter of fact. Instead they were required to discuss the controversial nature of the decision, to debate its merits in a matter-of-factly kind of way, which was built into the assessment task.

A year later they were required to role-play an encounter between an 'Aboriginal group' and 'pastoralists' in which they were the pastoralist who, according to the script, 'didn't want any trouble' from those trouble-making Aborigines. Here we can see how the education system insists to the Aboriginal child that they accept the 'inferiority of his [sic] culture',[11] that the rights long fought for were somehow still up for discussion, that even the verdict of their own highest court might not be right.[12] I guess it must be pretty unsettling for the coloniser to have one of their own institutions entertain the idea that the very foundations for its existence might be null and void.

Meanwhile, the terms by which the Aboriginal child is assessed academically is through their ability to articulate themselves as undeserving of their own land. That the Aboriginal child is forced into sympathising with, and standing in solidarity with, the coloniser standpoint speaks to the epistemic violence of colonial educational institutions. It is telling that the parenting capabilities of the Black parent too are assessed upon our willingness to expose our children to the daily violence of classrooms that are indoctrinating them with an Indigenousness that is deemed undeserving and unbelonging. They call it 'unexplained absence'.

because racism[13]

Walter Putnam notes how 'representation stands in for absence'.[14] Indeed, colonial representations of Aboriginal culture work to sustain absence, the lie of Terra Nullius. The false binary that Distinguished Professor Aileen Moreton-Robinson speaks of, of the traditional-modern Aborigine,[15] invokes culture, namely the culturally-lost or culture-less Aborigine, in the same way the 'doomed race destined to die out' once did. It is via culture that Indigenous rights to land are determined and, too, diminished. We only need look at the work of the anthropologists who are the arbiters of both our culture and our access to our own land, even when so many of their accounts have been proven flawed and false.

Working in a university Indigenous student support unit, I would witness the annual intake of Blackfullas enrolling in anthropology degrees at university for the sole purpose of getting their land back. It wasn't that long ago that Blackfullas would flock to law degrees to get land back, but I guess they soon realised that it was the anthropologists who had the power; precisely because they were the experts on *our* culture. It was the anthropologist's account that would be contested most among families but accepted uncritically in the coloniser's court. I would often end up providing support to those same students who stormed out of lecture theatres and tutorials having had their cultural story erased as part of the ongoing epistemic violence central to the colonisers' institutions. Culture, just like 'the native' who claimed to possess it, was always and only ever deemed to be dying or, in our account of it, deemed to be lying.

We can see these fictions in anthropology, a discipline founded in this place on the notion that our culture was dying and needed capturing before it passed. They flocked to communities in faraway places rather than to those that were being decimated by colonial violence. Here a pure and pristine culture could be captured, much like those real Aborigines that Australians claim to know, who provide the reference point for knowing and erasing the Aborigines they live among.

On the odd occasion that the anthropologist ventured to the city or a mission/reserve community, it was with a view to assist the state in absorbing the Aborigine into the white coloniser population. They typically found that 'the native's' capacity to assimilate was hindered by white intolerance and the rejection of white fathers and their families of their own Black children. Despite rendering said children culture-less, these observers would marvel as an aside at the ability of even the lightest-skinned Aborigine to trace their Aboriginal genealogy back to precolonial times. Yet the conclusion stood: 'the Aborigine' in these parts could never be 'fully Aboriginal'.[16] Once upon a time Aboriginality could be explained away through a racist eugenics of supposed blood quantum – much the same way that the white kids did at school. Now, in their erasure of 'the Aborigine', they talk less of a diluted blood, but instead a lost culture.

Aboriginal artist Richard Bell explains the phenomenon of the anthropologist so accurately:

Aboriginal cultures throughout the World have been infested by plagues of Anthropologists down the Ages. Never more so than during the last three decades here in Australia. We have been the most studied creatures on earth. They KNOW more about us than we know about our selves. Should you ask an Aboriginal how they're feeling, the most appropriate answer would be 'Wait 'til I ask my Anthropologist.' They are stuck so far up our arses that they [are] on first name terms with sphincters, colons and any intestinal parasites. And behold, the[y] DO speak for us.[17]

Who can forget the 'scholarly debates' of the 1990s where primarily white scholars published their feelings in peer-reviewed journals about which form of Aboriginality was most acceptable? And it was not just the domain of the anthropologist. The archaeologist, the linguist, the writer, the art dealer, the television producer, hell, even the pimply faced kid in my Year 9 class could insist that they were the only true purveyors of our culture. It is they who named us Aborigines and ever since they have insisted, much like the schoolteacher in Toni Morrison's *Beloved*, that 'definitions belong to the definers – not the defined'.[18]

It really is a peculiar situation to be situated in the land in which you became human, only to suffer coloniser conversations in classrooms and tearooms in which they muse over your humanity and your existence, when they know damn well that it is they who do not belong to this place. It is quite something that they could still maintain the power to decide what it is to *be* Aboriginal, and the terms on which it is culturally sufficient enough for us to have our land returned. I mean how and when did we supposedly lose our culture? I am yet to find the year when that took place – when did we forget? When did we relinquish our knowing of ourselves?

i'm not afraid of the dark[19]

I was raised in a home in which 'never forget who you are and where you come from' was almost a daily mantra, where Black people were sought out and sought after, whether that was via the occasional Black artist or film on television, the family reunions, the Black families on our street over several generations who became family, or the Black family members from out of town who occupied makeshift beds in our lounge room throughout our lives. I knew Blackness not only as a matter of living – I knew it to be strong, funny, silly, fierce, proud, beautiful.

It wasn't until I got to university that I came to realise how sick our state was as a people – beyond that of my own deviant behaviours in high school. I studied an undergraduate applied health science degree focused on Indigenous health, with a predominantly Indigenous cohort of students of varying ages. And together we learnt from white lecturers how ill, how tragic, how risky and problematic our existence was. It was a genuine shock to me to learn how sick we were as a people because, at our kitchen table, I was regaled with stories about Aunty Dora, for instance, who as a child was rounded up like cattle and brought to Brisbane from her traditional country up in the gulf region – but the story wasn't a tragic story, even though it was. The ending was that she lived to be over a hundred years of age. The moral of the story, its function in my dad retelling it over and over again, was to remind us of the strength of Black people despite the violence of white people. Dad would never say that explicitly, but it was the terms of reference for how we came to know ourselves in this place, one of outliving white violence rather than a survival predicated upon white benevolence.

Within the health sciences, we are not known as genocide survivors. We are unknown as living, as healthy, or as well. We are instead known via our premature deaths, via illness and ailments, the cause of which can be explained through a knowing of us as a people who don't know what's good for us.

And, if by some chance we did, we don't actually care about our health, and as such are undeserving of appropriate health care or the conditions for better health because we won't make the best use of those investments anyway.

When former Prime Minister Tony Abbott declared this continent 'nothing but bush',[20] he tapped into the colonial-settler sentiment whereby the land was for taking because we weren't making the best use of it. Under this logic, we too are determined incapable of and undeserving of the proper use of colonial institutions and systems. Instead we are told by the colonisers that 'the dying race' actually want to die earlier of almost every condition for which they have data on. It is why 'discharge against medical advice' is reported on in annual Closing the Gap reports and not the systemic failure of the health system. Just like 'unexplained school absenteeism', it is those damn Black people who are to blame.

Of course, in the classroom I sat in, much like the kitchen table I was fed at, Black people contested these claims every day in our being, and our thinking. It was this disjuncture between the stories we were told about us and the ones we told each other that led me to do a PhD. I wasn't trying to become an academic, having experienced academia's violence; I just wanted to tell a different story of Indigenous peoples that did justice to the stories we tell. In my desire to correct the record, I naively thought that if I just produced the evidence base on their terms in their house, then maybe things could change.

Audre Lorde had warned us of the uselessness of the master's tools[21] but sadly I didn't encounter her scholarship in the Indigenous health degree I was enrolled in, despite its commitment to the liberation of Blackfullas via better health. I encountered few Black or Indigenous scholars during this time and we were not taught about race and sovereignty. We were taught how to monitor Black bodies, to master the tools for surveillance, to measure blood pressures, HbA1cs, heart rate, health behaviours, risks and diseases. It was the ailing Black body that we were taught to know and to surveil.

So my resistance was to talk of strength, to refuse the logic that insisted Blackness and wellness were mutually exclusive and that our apparent illness was not a product of Black lack. My PhD findings claimed a 'discovery' of Indigeneity as understood by Indigenous peoples, which had nothing to do with illness and/or risk of it, but rather was central to our understanding of wellness.[22] And while the work did do something towards shifting imaginings of Indigeneity within public health, particularly in advancing strength-based approaches, it came at a cost, which I continue to pay to this day, particularly when I shifted from speaking of our identity, our culture and our strength, to speaking about race, whiteness and the violence of the health system.

This is why despite the academic medal, the dean's commendation, the national lifetime achievement award, research grants and keynotes within my discipline, I was not located within my discipline; not even at its margins. I remember once being permitted for a minute to sit in another school that was neither health nor population health. But even then, I didn't actually occupy an office on either of the floors that it takes up in the building. Instead I was placed in an office two floors further up, in a rented room on another school's floor and each day I walked two flights of stairs to collect my lunch from the tearoom or my photocopying from the printer. I did have a printer in my office but getting the ink cartridge replaced presented all kinds of challenges for the administrative staff. So, I would take the stairs. As a Blackfulla I am used to having to walk further and work harder. I don't know if I would even feel comfortable at the same table, let alone on the same floor as my supposed peers, which included those archaeologists, anthropologists, criminologists and other social scientists responsible for the racist knowledges produced about us, which have inflicted and continue to inflict violence upon Aboriginal people.

But there is also something really sick about the situation of Indigenous peoples as described within the health sciences, which consistently insists that we accept the inferiority of our culture. And that the very ideological foundation upon which we become visible is as statistically inferior – on terms of their choosing yet again. And despite over a decade of policy failure we are being subjected to a refresh of those statistical 'targets' rather than a radical reframing.[23] Despite my intellectual labouring in health, often at its margins, the centre remains intact. I guarantee you that there is not one Indigenous health research question drafted anywhere in this place, by an undergraduate, postgraduate student or principal investigator, that doesn't effectively ask, 'So what is wrong with Aboriginal people?'

I remember getting some respite, for a moment, teaching critical Indigenous studies out of an Indigenous studies unit away from the health and social sciences schools. Importantly I wasn't teaching the 1970s Aboriginal studies version that the anthropologists and archaeologists constructed, of artefacts and ancientness. I taught the 'Aboriginal people must be your source for your claims' kind of Indigenous studies built by Indigenous scholars locally and globally, the one that made room for talking about race inasmuch as it talked about culture.[24]

Here I could bring in texts by Aboriginal people and they didn't have to be clinicians, anthropologists or epidemiologists mimicking white expertise. They just had to be Black, and in fact there was room for all kinds of Blackness: the funny, the beautiful, the angry, the poetic, the political, all those shades that I had known growing up. I could think about my being through song, fictional texts, poetry, protest signs, all kinds of ways.

It was 'a peculiar sensation'[25] to think of oneself via possibilities rather than risk; to theorise rather than be pathologised. I think this is why the Indigenous academic, regardless of their disciplinary training, finds a home in Indigenous studies at some point in their career. It is not because we can't hack it in a mainstream faculty and those damn stairs we are forced to climb. It is that critical Indigenous studies is one of the few intellectual homes in which we get to exist in the here and now, as real and lived, as knowers not just known. And for the most part, I was 'good in the hood';[26] at least I thought so. It was from critical Indigenous studies that I was able to create an intellectual home for the work that I and others were doing, which bridged the divide between, while attending to the violence of, both health and humanities. This place is called Indigenist health humanities.[27]

I'm not for a minute suggesting that the humanities are any more of a safe haven than the health sciences. While the health sciences were all too happy to bury the bodies of a dying race, the humanities pillaged our graves in search of the remnants of a dying culture; some would have us skinned alive.[28] Having been shifted to the margins of the social sciences in among the anthropologists, archaeologists and criminologists, I realised how nothing had changed; how some days that office outside of the school's actual footprint in the building gave me the sense that my home did, a safety in being away from the place where the stockwhips get cracked, bones collected, and Black bodies flayed.[29]

Yet that building I was once based in is home to an anthropology museum located on the bottom floor. Each day as I marched up and down those stairs I couldn't help but think of my own footprint and what it was I was forced to step on each day. My sixth-floor office also offered a vantage point that overlooked the sandstone building that frames the great court of one of the nation's 'elite' universities. That building is engraved with Aboriginal people including Aboriginal heads, which at the time signified the flora and fauna that most Australians were described as being unfamiliar with.[30]

But my time in that ivory tower didn't last too long. Upon receiving a prestigious research grant that provided five years of my salary to build Indigenist health humanities as a new field of research, I found there was even less room available. I scoured spaces within the faculty in which the work could be situated, only to be told there was no room for the $1.77 million investment. I was shipped back to the Aboriginal studies unit, the place where the institution felt the work belonged, but which also had no actual physical space to accommodate me or my growing team. The school I was leaving was unable to provide me with any boxes to pack up my office, but with the help of colleagues I got out of there. I loaded my belongings into my car and had to transport them to my actual home, having no office to move in to. It was a peculiar sensation to find that, having secured the resources to exercise Indigenous intellectual sovereignty, there was absolutely no room at the inn, even in the 'hood I was returning to.

Sometimes I would ask myself, 'What am I doing *here*?' My eight years of undergraduate and postgraduate study within that institution, even in its excellence, did nothing to remedy that sense of unbelonging to that place. I will never forget the sense of indignation of a member of the senior executive when they asked me why I thought I 'belonged' in *their* faculty. It was as though they had thought that I had forgotten my place. But they did not realise that I had never accepted the place that the colonisers have reserved for us, that supposed place of unbelongingness. My answer to their question thus was not an appeal for inclusion, but an assertion of my sovereignty as an Indigenous scholar who had to remind them of whose land they were on.

Native American scholar Vine Deloria Jr declared, 'the problems of Indians have always been ideological rather than social, political or economic ... So it is vitally important that the Indian people pick the intellectual arena as the one in which to wage war'.[31] The war that I am interested in waging does not involve appealing to the colonisers to be seen, as human or healthy. Instead I am more concerned with those 'warring ideals in one dark body'[32] and minimising the violence inflicted upon it.

I want my children to see themselves and to know themselves beyond colonial caricatures, which insist we are incomplete, and inauthentic. I still remember Aunty Mary Graham talking about the important work that has yet to be done in finding ways to describe ourselves to each other. Frantz Fanon, too, talks of the emergence of a national consciousness,[33] perhaps the true one Du Bois thought eluded Black folk. This consciousness is not concerned with charming or resisting our oppressor but in speaking to one's own people, which he argues is a literature of combat because it 'moulds the national consciousness, giving it form and contours and flinging open before it new and boundless horizons; it is a literature of combat,' he says, 'because it assumes responsibility, and because it is the will to liberty expressed in terms of time and space'.

My work as an intellectual, 'native', 'Black', 'public' or otherwise, is not to be of service to the coloniser and their institutions. I am all too conscious of the limitations of what the academy can offer both the 'native' and 'the native intellectual'. I care little about sustaining the institution that exists to insist upon our non-existence. I am interested in what we might take from it and how I might wrest some of that academic freedom afforded the scholar to speak to each other. In the course of such acts, we must be careful not to get caught or caught up in the domestic duties they insist we occupy our time with.

I remember Mum telling me about my great-grandmother, known to us as 'Nanna Slockee'. As a young woman Nanna Slockee received an exemption from the Act in the 1920s, but the only role available to her was still that of domestic. In her later years, no longer in such work, Nanna Slockee would still ready herself for the day ahead, hair pinned back and apron on. Mum said she would always put that apron on to meet the day. How might we escape this role of servitude in our being? How might we know ourselves beyond the role that they have assigned us? How do we know ourselves as relating to each other amid the ongoing violence we are subject to, in ways that nourish us as Blackfullas?

i see deadly people[34]

I remember one of the times I felt there could be something nourishing about being a Black academic. It was a small research project that focused on Indigenous men's identity in partnership with a community organisation I am on the board of,[35] and which was accountable to an Indigenous men's governance process. This work was to explore a rites of passage process within the community to which I belonged, which had also been known to a television audience as 'struggle street'.[36]

43

This work would culminate in a documentary that followed the story of a group of young men. The frame of reference for this documentary was an Indigenous masculinity as described by 'original Inala boys', which included the ones we love and the ones we raise.

We didn't construct a problem that our research would solve; instead we wanted the research to tell the story from which we could learn, because we would listen. We didn't employ research officers to go collect data to define, measure and validate what a strong Indigenous masculinity could be, that they could aspire to; instead we used the money to engage a production team to film everything. They were given a brief. We told them not to film shopping trolleys on traffic islands. We told them to capture the beauty of the place and its people, and capture the beauty of this story, of the here and now. Even in combat, and particularly in combat, we must never forget how beautiful Blackfullas are. After all, that was the narrative arc of almost every story told at our kitchen table.

I remember filming the interviews with the original Inala boys in one sitting, one after the other. I remember most interviews involving laughter, tears and those damn goose-bumps that run the full length of your arm. It was special, and I remember driving home so excited by the stories so generously shared, and I knew the stories were rich because we did not assess their knowing: we centred it and amplified it. When we ask different questions, it is amazing what different stories get told. I remember being struck by the beauty, vulnerability, humour and intimacy of these men, not because I didn't know it but because, as an academic and a Blackfulla, rarely had I been permitted to know it or speak of it.

I still remember the screening of the documentary to our community before it went to air. After it stopped, it was really quiet and I had never been so nervous before. That silence lasted what felt like an eternity. One of the mothers finally stood up and said, 'We know that is our community, that is Inala and that is the Civic but I've never seen us look like this before.' It truly is a peculiar sensation watching people look in the mirror and be stunned by their own beauty, and not because they didn't know it themselves, but they never saw their beauty reflected back to them and for others to see.

This reaction made me rethink my reading of my daughter's drawing. Yes, there was a trope that was reproduced and that reflected the colonial representation of a 'culturally pure Aborigine'. Yet unlike those glossy project cards at my newsagency, she was able to narrate us into a place. She and her siblings were named and her depiction demanded that she explain who she was and where she came from in terms of why her family appeared as both animals and elements. That picture required her to tell a story of her presence via a language that locates her to the place in which our people became human. And I realised the significance of the gift that we had given to her as her parents: the gift of knowing, of locating oneself in relation to country in our account of ourselves, even within a colonial institution that kept telling her not to.

still here[37]

The 'problem of the Aborigine' in the colony is our very presence; always was, always will be. Despite the colonisers' best efforts to disperse 'the Aborigine' geographically or absorb us statistically, we remain, and we continue to claim a being via our land and our culture, rather than via a proximity to them. It is in our presence that we remind them that we are 'still here' despite their daily insistence that we only exist in a land far, far away, in a faraway time. We do not speak of being *there*, we speak of being *here*, because their notion of *there* is a nowhere place, somewhere in the Territory or the Cape, but never really specified. Our inability to fit within the category or location of 'Aborigine', as defined by them, is not a limitation of our identity or a failing of our communities; it is emblematic of the strength of Indigenous sovereignty, a steadfast refusal to comply with the claim of unbelongingness they have tried to attach to our bodies and our stories.

Dispossession, you see, is more than the stuff of land.

In the colony, Blackfullas are forced to embody an illusory double-consciousness between existing and non-existing, human and non-human, real and unreal, traditional and modern. It is more than a peculiar sensation; it is a dispossessing location. But it is via Indigenous sovereignty that we contest this false consciousness, most notably in our stubborn claim of 'still here'. Still here is a short-form way of saying 'sovereignty never ceded'. This phrase finds itself on Black bodies, on belt buckles and T-shirts, etched on tourist signs and Facebook memes, song titles and on protest banners from cities to shorelines. It is a refusal to subscribe to the myth of our demise. But 'still here' is not an appeal to be seen; it represents a victory lap for Blackfullas, a fierce reminder to the colonisers that they didn't succeed; never have and never will.

Despite our supposed marginal status, statistically and culturally, the Black body itself is not marginalised. It is powerful, in its remembering, in its standing still – here. We exist not on boundaries, between binaries, or a dual consciousness, but fully, here, and fully human. Moreton-Robinson reminds us that, in life and in death, Black bodies testify to the truth of this place, signifying our 'title to this land'.[38] As such, we are not situated on a frontline; rather, it is the Black body that *is* the frontline. It is our bodies upon which colonial violence is visited most brutally, and that is why I come to health as a Blackfulla – not to remedy our condition behaviourally or materially to stave off disease. I come to health to strategise a Black living which presumes a Black future, of a forevermore kind; a future that doesn't mark itself via an aspirational proximity to colonisers, of a 'vanishing Aborigine' via gap closing, but one that is set on our terms, on our lands. It is on those terms that we mark out the battleground on which we are prepared to fight, but too provide the necessary armour for those who in their sovereign Black selves put their lives on the line every damn day in the colony.

2

animals, cannibals and criminals

Juvenile Justice Act 1992
Section 12 (1)
Section 17 (1)
QUEENSLAND

O.P.B. 62
7/93

Certificate of Caution

Family Name: *WATEGO*　　　Given Names: *Chelsea Joanne*

Residential Address:　　　Postcode:

Date of Birth:　　　Place of Birth:

Offence Details

Time: *12·15* am/pm　Date: *12·9·93*　CO Number

Location: *Platform 1 Myer Centre Bus Terminal*　Postcode: *4000*

Offence Title: *Assaults occasioning bodily harm*　Statute: *Crim Code*　Section: *339*

Number of offences for which caution administered: *ONE*　(Details of further offences overleaf)

In respect of the within offence/s a caution has been administered under Section 12(1) of the Juvenile Justice Act 1992.

Caution Details

Date: *29·9·93*　Police Establishment where caution administered: *Juvenile Aid, Mt Gravatt*

Persons Present - Other than Authorised Officer and Child:

Family Name: *WATEGO*　　　Given Names

Person administering caution:

Family Name　　　Given Names　　　Rank and Reg. No.

Authorised Officer Present during Caution:

Name　　　Rank and Reg. No.　　　Signature of Auth.

NOTICE:　A caution is an official process authorised by Division 2 of the Juvenile Justice Act 1992. The caution is designed to make you aware of the consequences of unlawful actions; to make you aware of rights, responsibilities and obligations under the law; and to reinforce the notion of you being responsible for your actions. It is hoped that the administration of a caution to you will divert you from committing further offences and the Court's criminal justice system. A caution is administered to you instead of placing you before a court.

The Juvenile Justice Act 1992 requires that, at the conclusion of the caution, you be provided with a *Certificate of Caution*. You are requested to retain this *Certificate of Caution* as it may be produced to show that you have been dealt with for the above offence/s. The administration of a caution means that you are not liable to be prosecuted at a later time for the above offence/s.

Acknowledgement

1. I consent to being cautioned for *ONE* offence/s.
2. I admit committing the offence/s.
3. I acknowledge that a police caution has been administered to me for the above offence/s.
4. I acknowledge receiving a *Certificate of Caution*.

Child　　　Witness　　　Authorised Of

Print witness name

Thus the labor of race is the work for which the category
and its assumptions are employed to effect and rationalize
social arrangements of power and exploitation, violence and
expropriation. Race was turned into a foundational code. But
as with all foundations (conceptual and material), it had to be
cemented in place. Racial thinkers, those seeking to advance racial
representation – scientists and philosophers, writers and literary
critics, public intellectuals and artists, journalists and clergy,
politicians and bureaucrats – for all intents and purposes became
the day-laborers, the brick-layers, of racial foundations.

David Theo Goldberg[1]

Once upon a time, you could go to the school library and find any number of books about the Aborigine. These books typically were located in the children's fiction section and included colourful dreamtime stories about our creation all under the banner of myths and fables,[2] except they were always from an unstated elsewhere place. And yes, you could occasionally find mention of us in the reference section, typically as a people from the past, of ancientness and artefacts. It was as though ideologically we were positioned somewhere between the Loch Ness monster and the ancient pyramids, complete with the mystery of our existence, in how we came to be, whether we still really existed and who had actually sighted us.

These days when you arrive at the Indigenous section of a library or bookshop, you will find the preponderance of texts situated in the non-fiction section. These are typically not authored by the Aborigine but still make all kinds of claims to know 'them'. In this era of a supposed 'new paternalism'[3] and mainstreaming in Indigenous affairs that greeted us at the turn of the century, we see fewer texts about the culturally authentic Aborigine, about the dreamtime stories and basket weaving of my childhood, and more of the Aboriginal-as-problem type texts. Such texts have been around for some time and are most definitely not new, but their dominance in this time reflects where 'the Aborigines' exist right now in the 'settler consciousness'.[4]

Within the current Indigenous social policy context of gap closing,[5] the Aborigine is constructed as a problem; a problem that can be solved statistically, through increased control and surveillance by the state. So, naturally, they need texts which simultaneously construct us as the problem and themselves as the solution. I'm reminded of Gomeroi scholar Alison Whittaker's searing book review[6] of a coloniser's text in which she wrote: 'I'm reading this book everywhere I go. That's not an endorsement, but it is an observation.' For me, she was not speaking of just one text but speaking to our encounter with the 'Aboriginal as problem' genre that is so widely lauded by the colonisers.

Ironically, this so-called Aboriginal genre rarely seems to include an Aboriginal protagonist. In the fictional story the protagonist is always a well-intentioned coloniser who cares more about 'the Aborigines' than they do about themselves, even the Black mothers who birthed them, who are increasingly depicted as absent. In not belonging to someone or somewhere, 'the Aborigine' is made free for the taking.[7] In the non-fiction texts, the white protagonist is the author who can speak candidly about 'the Aborigines' they encountered, while never being accountable to those they write about.

'The Aborigine' is never cast as a character, but instead appears as the conflict; it is in our supposed culture and inherently violent disposition that 'the Aborigine' appears. There never is a happy ever after for 'the Aborigines'; happy endings are always reserved for the colonisers and are achieved through a supposedly reluctant resignation to the 'fact' of a doomed race destined to die, at some time or another. 'The Aboriginal problem' is always solved via the demise of 'the Aborigine' and/or its culture. And, we are assured, it is all of their own making, much like when Jedda joined 'the greater mother of the world, in the dreaming time of tomorrow'.[8]

Aboriginal people have long mused over the texts we have encountered about us, because in their speaking their lies about us, we were summoned to speak truth. Some Blackfullas became poets, some became playwrights, some became journalists, some became teachers, some became lawyers and some became academics, often with the immediate goal of correcting the account, not as critics or complainants, but as authors – as knowers. Despite being armed with our degrees, our titles, our theories, our literary awards and our research grants, we simply could not be believed. Our work was deemed biased, emotive, political, passionate and radical, and despite how moving and articulate the account, the Aboriginal author could never be cast as all-knowing like the 'white witness'.[9]

The power of the white witness is not in their literary capabilities, but rather in their willingness to sustain coloniser mythologising of 'the Aboriginal problem'. This is not just about the stories they tell, but their location. For the coloniser mythologies about the Aborigine are never in the children's or fiction section – they stand exclusively in the non-fiction area, for it is their account that is always 'fact'.

Some are even called courageous. There are any number of books written by white playwrights, magistrates, teachers, film directors and anthropologists who in their 'day-labouring'[10] around race tell all kinds of fanciful tales of Black violence and white benevolence. The Aboriginal writer meanwhile is permitted to feel, but not think.[11] That is why there is room for the Aboriginal author to tell fictional tales about 'the Aborigine' and it is they who you will see on the writers' festival circuit telling their tales to white audiences. The Black author who refuses to 'admit the inferiority of his [sic] culture'[12] in their writing, who shifts the location of their text from fiction to non-fiction, to write of facts instead of fables, refusing to narrate the account of 'the Aboriginal problem', will find themselves with all sorts of problems, even with their own publisher. The Aborigine in their written testimony can only ever authorise and accessorise coloniser mythologies – they can never theorise their existence. Well, mostly.

fact or fiction?

I remember the first time I was invited to a writers' festival, at the invitation of curator Sisonke Msimang. I had the opportunity to be a panellist and do a live *Wild Black Women* radio show. I also was invited to provide a keynote address, the 'Randolph Stow Lecture', no less. The lecture was not so much an opportunity to speak of my own writing, but to comment on the life and work of Stow, which I was to learn was an annual tradition at the festival.

Now until this time I wasn't familiar with the life and work of Stow and I tried to read one of his books, *To the Islands*, only because I had been told by one of the organisers that it had won a Miles Franklin and included the oral testimony of Daniel Evans who had recited a massacre story. They had assured me that Stow was supportive of Indigenous people, but had cautioned of some problematic elements to this story. My inclusion as the keynote was framed as making a space for an Indigenous voice to speak back to Stow. So I tried to read the book.

The book is centred around the white protagonist's 'agonised search for a home in an alien universe',[13] and includes a fictionalised account of the Forrest River Massacre. Stow, we are advised at the start of the book, 'engages powerfully the guilt that haunts the descendants of those responsible for such killings', and which apparently haunts the main character who devotes his life to making reparations.[14] It was strange to me that there wasn't some reference to the significance of this most brutal massacre upon the Aboriginal characters, even in a revised edition in 2002. How could it be that an actual massacre of Aboriginal people by white men could be repurposed for a fictional story simply for examining how it had haunted white men?

It was stunning to me the swiftness with which white violence could be transformed into white guilt without having restored any justice, dignity or humanity to the Aboriginal men, women and children most affected by the brutality of colonisation. One would think the violence and trauma experienced by Blackfullas could be an opportunity for crafting more 'well-rounded'[15] complex Black characters as opposed to humanising colonisers.

Interestingly, Stow provides a preface to his revised edition in which he declares the book's many faults – the faults related to his own immaturity and technical incompetence. Yet he unashamedly claims that the original account was, in his words, 'consciously making propaganda on behalf of Christian mission-stations for Aborigines, in particular for one Mission on which I had worked for a short time'.[16] Here we see the function of the fiction so very clearly in the author's own words. Through a fictional story based on his own experience, Stow creatively constructs an alternative truth that is less about the attempted reparations of one white man, and more a story of redemption for white men serving the colonial project.

Stow, in his preface, goes on to explain that writers before him had given missions and missionaries bad press, but at least one of these was doing good and thus must be defended, he claimed. After all, we are cautioned, the community might not exist except for the charity of the Church of England and its servants. Again, it was bizarre to me that the solution to the problem of colonial settlerism would be a continuation of colonial control which is re-narrated as inherently benevolent rather than inherently violent.

Whittaker helps make sense of this in her critique of Sarah Maddison's non-fiction text *The Colonial Fantasy*, which it could be argued is one of the more sympathetic works to the plight of Indigenous people in our time. Whittaker points out that 'even when the Australian public "gets" the idea of Indigenous sovereignty, the right to monitor its efficacy and the claim to benevolence and legitimacy remains'. 'Our sovereignty,' she writes, 'becomes a colonial benevolence, a supervised gift to us that bolsters their legitimacy.'[17] But our sovereignty was never ceded, so it cannot be given to us by the colonisers. Sadly, the colonisers cannot see a way out of their relationship to us and this place that is not predicated upon their control over us.

Stow, of course, was not interested in the unceded sovereignty of Indigenous peoples but instead was explicitly making a case for maintaining the 'colonial logic of managerialism' that Whittaker suggests Maddison too can't see her way out of,[18] a logic in which the answer is a more effectively managed colony rather than decolonisation.

In his preface Stow boasts that his book was mentioned in parliament as a brilliant story – massacre and all, it seems. He laments that the mention was not in relation to maintaining the mission or increasing resourcing to it; instead the book was used to make a case for professors of Australian literature. The result was the invention of Chairs and the abandonment of the mission. We see here a desperate need to create an Australian literary canon that would further cement the idea of Australian nationhood. White authors writing about Black people, fictional or factional, are never just narrating good or true stories – they are always philosophising about the architecture of Indigenous affairs, which always concludes with a rationalisation of white control, narrated as charitable.

Take, for instance, Stow in his preface, where he continues to tell us of the catastrophic consequences of the abandonment of the mission/reserve system for the supposed fictional community. Now I cannot speak for the actual community on which this story was based. It isn't my place to speak of that story. I can guarantee that within my own state of Queensland you will find mob who talk fondly of the mission days not because they believe necessarily that missions or reserves were the solution but that, even in the most oppressive conditions, our mob exercised agency in these places, finding meaning in hardship, never relinquishing our humanity or our humour.[19] And, of course, we all can look fondly at a past in which some of the challenges we face today were not a problem. But the thing is, association is not cause. And there are some really problematic causal relationships being articulated in coloniser fictions about our mob.

As Jeanine Leane points out in her analysis of *Coonardoo*, 'It struck me that thousands of years of Aboriginal culture and spirituality were being reduced to base instinct.'[20] Coonardoo and her fellow Aboriginal women were cast as victims of their own rampant sexuality; it was their animalistic desires that destroyed them. The colonial scheme imposed on these Aboriginal women was presented as justified; it was to 'save' them from themselves.

It is important to recognise that the typically savage and animalistic depictions of Aboriginal characters in Australian literature are not merely found in texts produced at a certain moment, a moment that is always described as 'of its time'. Those fictions serve a function. The insistence that the world's oldest living continuing culture is incapable of existing as a functioning society without white control is a fictional narrative constructed by the colonisers that finds itself cemented as the canon of Australian literature – precisely because it affirms the presence of a people who came to this place on the false promise and premise of our non-existence. These fanciful tales soothe the coloniser's guilt about their own violent illegal occupation. Australian literature works for the coloniser (author, reader and publishing house) as that soothing bedtime story that puts the unsettled child to sleep by insisting that 'the native' really needs them after all.

Stow in his preface to the revised edition goes so far as to insist that the fictional massacre in his book had a positive effect on race relations because of the generosity of the superintendent, Gribble, upon whom this book is based. We are reminded of the enlightened attitudes of the Church evidenced by one white man in one community as opposed to the murdering policemen. Stow laments that the affectionate relations between Black and white may not be seen again for at least a generation or two.

Now I am not discounting the reality that Gribble was an outspoken advocate against the violence and exploitation of Aboriginal men, women and the children, for which he paid a price, nor am I objecting to the idea that this is an important story to tell. It is, however, most bizarre that the feats of one white man became the fictional centrepiece in a very real story of everyday and ongoing colonial violence.

How is it that Stow ignores any possible relationship between colonial violence and the social conditions of Aboriginal communities at that time or now? And in what time is it acceptable to suggest that a massacre could have been a good thing for race relations? I guess, if 'race relations' is really code for redeeming the role of white men as virtuous rather than violent, then any time is fine. After all, Stow is making this claim in 1991.

And there I was at page nine. I hadn't yet got to the story. Yet, despite my best efforts, I just couldn't read the story. I already knew the violent function of this literary genre. It has not just functioned to make stories that white writers can sell and carve out careers from; it has served the colonial project more loyally than 'the native' characters contained within them ever could.

This literary genre in stretching across fiction and non-fiction typically blurs the boundaries between the two. The fictions are claimed as fact by the white author who has engaged in what Whittaker refers to as 'intellectual tourism into our alleged dysfunction'.[21] It is not uncommon for these texts to emerge from an experience that the white author has had in a professional context (of which creative writing was not the skill set). After just a few months or a few years in an Aboriginal community they become literary geniuses, on the speaking circuit having praise heaped on them for (1) being charitable enough to mix with 'the native folk' in 'the tropics' and (2) for having solved a problem, even if that solution is simply a more creative retelling of the same tired story. And, of course, it is always the problematic, treacherous, dysfunctional, cannibalistic, criminal 'native' who props up the poor plot.

'The kind of engagements *The Colonial Fantasy* invites are also not really the fault of the author as much as they are symptoms of a settler-centric industry,' Whittaker explains. 'Colonisation and settler authority is parasitically enmeshed with every part of non-Indigenous and Indigenous lives.'[22] Indeed, what industry in this place can't trace its origins and/ or its ongoing survival to the exploitation of Black lives, lands or labour? I'm not talking simply about mining, sheep or sugar; I'm talking about industries such as anthropology founded upon knowing 'the native' and sustained by knowing that 'native's' land better than we can know it ourselves. I'm talking about Australian literature, which insists upon writing better representations of us, despite not being grounded in our reality.

Leane[23] observed how Patrick White in *A Fringe of Leaves* readily constructed a fictional story of Aboriginal cannibals, not having met Aboriginal people. She also wrote of his claim that he didn't need to engage with Butchulla when visiting K'gari, also known as Fraser Island, because their account would complicate things. How ironic that the Black people from which the Black characters originate could get in the way of a supposed 'good story'.

The canon of Australian literature, we are reminded, is to be of service to the coloniser, not the colonised, and Black bodies get conjured up in the most vile and fanciful ways to aid it, with absolutely no accountability. Marcia Langton explained many years ago that:

> the densest relationship is not between actual people but between white Australians and the symbols created by their predecessors. Australians do not relate to Aboriginal people. They relate to stories told by former colonists ... The Aborigines that Australians 'know' are Bennelong, Jedda and Marbuk ... They are safe, distant distortions of an actual world of people who will not bring the neighbourhood real estate values down.[24]

Despite the denseness of this relationship, Whittaker's examination of the reception of *The Colonial Fantasy* revealed little self-reflection from the colonisers about the implication on their own lives and practices. She observed another telling silence, which was the absence of Indigenous-authored critiques of the text. This silence is not a matter of mob not speaking back.

Alexis Wright acknowledges that there has long been a storytelling war, but the problem she argues is that one party remains intent on continuing this battle.[25] And if you do the literary festival tours in this place, you will see the appetite for it in the curation, staging and performances. I've been in those audiences at writers' festivals where white people clamour to the front of Q and As to chastise the Indigenous author insisting they got it wrong, while the white author can sit on stage and muse about their lack of accountability to 'the natives' with not one woke progressive white woman questioning them. I've even been in audiences where the microphone runners stop handing the mic to 'cosmetically apparent'[26] Aboriginal audience members when they dare question the white author about the violent and false Black fiction they've constructed. And we all know about the supposedly provocative white female keynote who reduces Black critique to an issue of identity politics and free speech, or worse a violent and aggressive attack.[27]

Black critique is almost always read as an attack; it is rarely considered insightful or constructive. The Black critic is framed as the threat, not just to the white author, but also to creativity and freedom, it would seem. Yet it's the Black critic who is most at risk in these encounters. Author Roxane Gay has spoken of the weekly death threats she receives that require her to pay for a security service to monitor and protect her, and states, 'People need to realise what real censorship looks like. They need to understand how unsafe it can be to challenge authority and the status quo.'[28] She goes on to speak of the attacks against Wendy Ortiz who wrote an essay critiquing the novel *American Dirt*, which were largely from white women and, she argued, quite common. Gay states, 'We see this a lot in online discourse where people see something that triggers or upsets them, and they worry that it could happen to them someday. So they get behind whoever they perceive is the biggest victim, and it's always going to be the white woman.'

I haven't had death threats, but I deal constantly with triggered white women who insist they are victims of my truth-telling as a scholar. I haven't had to pay for extra security to protect my life, but I have paid a fair bit of money to explore how best to protect my family home. You see I have had several defamation threats come to my workplace as a scholar and a radio host, and at least three pieces of writing that were or still are in doubt of being published despite all being commissioned works.

the storytelling war

As previously mentioned, Fanon reminds us of the importance of a literature of combat; one that is concerned not with charming or resisting our oppressor, but one that addresses our own people, capable of moulding the national consciousness in fighting for our existence as a people.[29] But that isn't so easy if you are not prepared to tell the stories that don't fit within the narrow parameters of the 'colonial consciousness'.

There are any number of storytelling wars I have had in my life but I want to tell of the wars in the academy, the ideological war that Vine Deloria Jr speaks of.[30] I found myself in this war somewhat unwittingly. I came to the academy not to fight but to correct the account of us. As previously stated, I thought I could do that with an evidence base. But time and time again I was proven wrong – not via the evidence base I provided, but the strategy of thinking it was all a matter of evidence. Such a strategy was premised upon the idea that the coloniser just didn't know, and that if they heard our account or saw the evidence, they would accept it and act accordingly. I, too, mistakenly thought that as a Black academic I could speak to my own people, describing ourselves to each other the way Aunty Mary Graham[31] had spoken of. Yet even in speaking among ourselves, the colonisers always feature as both character and conflict, which they feel compelled to silence.

I am not convinced that white Australians have a difficult relationship with the stories told by their ancestors; the difficulty they have seems more to do with the stories that Aboriginal people tell of ourselves. You see when 'the natives' speak among ourselves, the colonisers always feel quite unsettled. Even those who 'lean in' to listen to our account of things will still relegate such accounts to either the history or mythology section in their mind. The Black story must be a site for which the coloniser can express sympathy, and not in a solidarity kind of way, but a condescending sorrow for our supposed plight. Our stories should not be repositories for which faux coloniser sympathy may find a home, yet too often they are.

I remember when I authored an opinion piece for *The Conversation* in response to the Bill Leak affair.[32] A cartoonist for the national broadsheet, Leak sought to distract attention from state-sanctioned violence against Aboriginal children in Don Dale Youth Detention Centre in the Northern Territory by suggesting it was the fault of Aboriginal fathers who don't know the names of their own offspring. I endeavoured to tell a more truthful account of the Indigenous dad: the one that I was reared by and the one who was rearing my children with me. But this was not just a personal testimony; I engaged with relevant literature to describe the discourse of the Black male perpetrator and its function in both historical and contemporary contexts.

It was a good piece and indeed it generated a decent readership and helped inspire the *Indigenous Dads* hashtag with the use of personal photographs of my children with their father. But behind this was a conflict between me and the editor who was sympathetic but concerned about 'balance' and 'facts'. I was advised to add a line and/or link to a report to show that some Aboriginal men do abuse their children. I was angered that there would be a sentence somewhere in this article, which included photographs of two of my children with their father in some intimate family moments, where readers would consider that he might potentially be a perpetrator.

There were some heated conversations. I refused to have it published if I was forced to include that line. Fortunately for me, on that occasion I won. I was permitted to tell my account of the Indigenous dads in my life and the racial violence that we had been – and continue to be – subjected to, but it wasn't easy. Had I not had a prior readership, and had I not so aggressively fought for the right to tell a story of the humanity of the Black men in my life, I might have authored a story that served the colonisers more than it did those Black men I was honouring.

Other times I haven't been so fortunate.

The first defamation threat I was subjected to was as a result of my public objection to my middle child being used in a campaign by the Queensland Department of Education, as a child who was, and I quote, one of 'the trouble-makers, the misunderstood, the kid that everyone thought wouldn't make it'.[33] The photo and accompanying narrative were used in an online campaign to encourage teachers (i.e. white women) to go and teach in rural and remote Queensland. So the department went to a suburban school with a high proportion of Aboriginal children, dressed them in lap-laps and ochre to pose with the white-presenting teacher. This image was taken a few years back but appeared on Indigenous Literacy Day.

Within hours the post was removed because of the response online and the media that ensued when it was revealed that one of those kids was the child of an academic, made apparent when I created a Twitter thread in response to the saga, which spoke in defence of the capabilities of my child and me as a parent who thought he would make it. I authored an article a little while later that included a reference to this event and I did an invited presentation at an education conference where I was asked to tell my story.

I didn't name individuals or blame them – in fact I used this as an opportunity to open up a dialogue for thinking about the ease with which these racialised narratives are attached to our children just in turning up to school.

Now I can't show you the picture in full, despite it still being publicly available, nor can I show you the Twitter thread that I posted because the institution that I worked for wanted this to go away and those were the conditions that I reluctantly conceded to. It's not like I wanted to get harassed at my job either, with relentless emails, or jeopardise my job, because the defamation threat didn't just come to me – the dean of my faculty was copied in on it.

I didn't concede to all the conditions, which included meeting face to face and vetoing any further scholarly outputs associated with this affair. But I had to remind the institution of my right to academic freedom and I sought out independent legal advice so I could advise the institutional legal department of how the law works and of my right to protection as a scholar, and my right to tell the truth about my child as his mother. The response letter from legal was one that I largely authored, because it was I who had to write my own defence. In their knowing of 'the Aborigine', the coloniser suddenly turns all kind of quiet when it comes to defending us, even when it is their job.

The outrageous thing about this affair is that it was me and my child who were framed as the troublemakers, yet our only crime was to be truth-tellers who still afforded those involved a fair degree of generosity. The image that my child was featured in is still being used for the same purpose of testifying to the importance of rural teaching in an article authored by the supposed real victim in all of this, albeit the Aboriginal children are now blurry figures in the backdrop.[34] They are the perfect kind of Aboriginal characters needed for this story, neither well-raised nor 'well-rounded'.[35] And there is nothing I can do about the use of my child for this purpose.

In that article, readers are advised:

Working in a remote community will change your teaching career, your perspective on life and, most importantly, you will understand and be able to contribute to conversations and political agendas with knowledge – not assumptions and influence from people who have never walked within a rural or remote community. These communities need voices that speak with truth.[36]

It is most interesting here the ways in which Aboriginal children are used as bait for white women to work in Black communities; one of the incentives, beyond the extra pay, is to be an authority in Indigenous affairs and political agendas.

I was invited to write an essay about this experience for a textbook around deficit discourse and the education system so I told the story about what happened to my child and the processes by which I was chastised and silenced for insisting upon my right to defend him as the Aboriginal mother. The editors were keen to include it in the book; however, the reviewer assigned to it had strong reservations.[37] The reviewer suggested my analysis as a critical race scholar writing about an experience of race was not undertaken in academic terms. They went on to insist on exercising caution on using the term 'white' because they felt I had used it as a proxy for ethnicity or race as opposed to phenotype. According to them, white wasn't a racial category or ethnic group but a physical description.

Apparently, this 'black/white binary' I deploy is problematic because according to the anonymous reviewer it didn't appear to account for fair-skinned Aboriginal people. They concluded that I should, therefore, review each instance of 'white'. It was suggested that I use 'non-Indigenous' instead of 'white' because apparently my experience relating to Black and white characters is reproducing the very oppression I am experiencing. It struck me that 'non-Indigenous' was seen as a legitimate racial category or ethnicity. I offered to again withdraw my essay rather than attend to the reviewer's whiteness. The editors advised they were prepared to accept it. Some two years later the text remains unpublished, as does my account of things as an Aboriginal mother and scholar.

Romaine Moreton, in speaking of the 'sovereign storyteller', reminds us that since time immemorial we have been great storytellers (despite what they say) and it is our stories that have 'kept a whole country humming for thousands of years through the power of our storytelling'.[38] This is why story, our stories, and our right to tell them must be defended, by any means necessary.

Story is life. And the colonisers' stories aren't stories committed to our living or our sovereignty, regardless of how benevolent they make the white protagonist. These exist always and only to protect the coloniser, sustaining the greatest fiction of them all – that of Terra Nullius, which is only made possible via race.

The racialised imaginings of Aboriginal characters, and the lengths white writers go to maintain their power to know and control 'the native population', are not of a time, but they are of a place: this place, here and now. A place where a non-colonising coexistence has yet to be realised, but where that resistance is supported and sustained by the Australian literary scene, which always gives greater weight to white fictions rather than the factual accounts of Blackfullas. A place which has yet to centre or celebrate sovereign storytellers; those who speak to the souls of Blackfullas rather than white women.

The Black witness, according to Amy McQuire,[39] is the Black women on the frontline who are doing the work here and everywhere, which is at greater cost than it is reward in such industries. Black women, you will find, are doing this work for the simple fact that it is our bodies and our babies that are being brutalised by white women who now dominate the literary and scholarly landscapes where we reside, or at least where we are trying to carve out a living. It is the Black mother who is narrated as absent, dysfunctional and the cause of the problems facing the Aboriginal children who are supposedly being rescued by the colonisers. The Aboriginal child in so many literary and cinematic representations finds themselves in the clutches of white women, often in an era when so many white fathers were denying the Aboriginal children they fathered, while the state was rationalising its right to steal them 'for their own good'.

In these accounts, our children are represented as 'remnants' of a people the colonisers needed to die out and it is the Black mother who has fought so viciously to reclaim the children we birthed and named, through the stories we tell of them. McQuire as sovereign storyteller reminds us that powerlessness is itself a fiction that they have narrated us in … but she reminds us, as do I, of the power of the Black woman as witness, most fierce, most factual, most scholarly and most generous. And it is these stories that should be told, read, heard and memorialised in this place, rather than the fictions of white folk and their fanciful psychological journeys.

If only they could be told.

Instead of the accounts we offer, we are offered their account of us. I first encountered the text *Saltwater* by Cathy McLennan[40] through several different Blackfullas who expressed surprise and anger about the contents of the book and its animalistic depictions of Aboriginal people. Others in the legal fraternity had raised questions about the author's public talks and appearances speaking about Indigenous health and social policy based on her book, which focused on a two-year stint in Townsville working with the Aboriginal and Islander Legal Service. Others had raised questions about her sentencing of Indigenous peoples as a magistrate in relation to sly grogging.[41]

As it would turn out, around the same time that I encountered *Saltwater* I was offered an invitation to contribute an article for a special edition of the *Australian Feminist Law Journal* that focused on 'Indigenous Writing on Law and Justice'. The theme was quite broad and open to my interpretation and could include discussions on sovereignty and systemic racism in the academy or any other issue related to the topic. I decided to focus my attention on *Saltwater* and the more I read and researched the book, the genre, the role of the author and the broader context in which it was published, the article started to write itself. It was submitted to the journal and subject to peer review. Both anonymous reviews were overwhelmingly supportive, with minor suggestions that I attended to.

Reviewer 1 stated:

I recommend this article be published as it makes a valuable contribution to Aboriginal scholarship in the fields of literary, cultural studies and the studies of writing and racial literacy ... Article presents a strong argument from an Aboriginal writer on the continuing cognitive imperialistic story-telling and the damage this does to real people. Judicious and thoughtful use of theorists and secondary material ...

Reviewer 2 noted:

This is a beautifully written – and wonderfully sardonic – engagement with the perpetuation of myth-making by non-indigenous people who make claims of and about indigineity in Queensland. Building on Behrendt's work on the mythologising fallacies of Eliza Fraser, the author then forensically pulls apart and unravels the narrations – and narcissisms – of a young Queensland magistrate who purports to account for indigeneity – as a supposedly sympathetic white lawyer. This was an uncomfortable pleasure to read – and a piece that needs to be widely distributed.

Sadly, the journal's managing editor and the editor-in-chief didn't share the same viewpoint as the anonymous reviewers or the special issue editors, Gomeroi scholar Alison Whittaker and Birri Gubba and Yugambeh scholar Dr Nicole Watson. The story of what transpired is documented elsewhere[42] but suffice to say after much back and forth, the managing editor and editor-in-chief advised that this work was not publishable in any form because it apparently posed a threat of defamation because the white woman author of the book I was critiquing wouldn't like my review.

The managing editor subjected the article to another peer-review process, which she undertook herself, without advising the special issue editors. She had lots of suggestions for the article that didn't relate specifically to the defamation threat. But her real concern was that there was an imputation that the author of the book was racist.

Now I didn't say the author was racist, but I did have about 180 footnotes, three-quarters of which were direct quotes from the text that cited animalistic references to the Aboriginal characters. When I queried the legal musings of the managing editor and her friend who she had sent my article to, who for the record stated he was legally unable to provide legal advice, I was accused of being ungrateful. Nonetheless I was advised that, regardless of whether the claims in the article were true or not, 'the reliance upon truth is very difficult in defamation law'.[43]

And this is at the heart of the storytelling war, and the dangers confronting the sovereign storyteller in the colony. We simply are not permitted to speak freely and truthfully about the violence we are subject to, not as mothers nor as scholars. Now unlike previous occasions, in this instance I had expressed a willingness to modify the work to minimise the risk. I felt the story of *Saltwater* and the function it served was too important to be kept silent. I eliminated almost a thousand words of text that were viewed as most problematic by the journal staff and was prepared to accept their insistence that it go through another peer-review process. Ironically the text that I eliminated, which I cannot speak to, was described by Reviewer 1 in the following terms: 'the beautiful unravelling of this behaviour is part of the power of this writing which is so compelling'.

I was eventually permitted to write an editorial about the experience of not being published in the special issue in lieu of the article I had submitted. But this would be accompanied with another contribution from a white man to explain how defamation law works at the insistence of the editor-in-chief. So, his 'voice of reason' appears in a special edition of Indigenous women's writing, to explain the exclusion of mine.

I resigned myself to the fact that the story wouldn't be told; in fact I had become accustomed to the silencing work of white women in the academy, but I was continually amazed at the need for the white woman to have the last say, even when she got her way. For instance, I was fortunate to have been invited to feature on the front cover of the special issue by the guest editors; however, it was around this time that journal editorial staff sought to impose yet another restriction. Now they were requesting that I remove any reference to the author or the book from the editorial that they had granted me. Fortunately that instruction was not supported, but the timing of this new rule and the lack of grounds for it were reminders that we are still embroiled in a storytelling war, whether fact or fiction.

I should note that some three months after having been advised that my article was not publishable in any form, I received correspondence advising that members of the editorial board of the journal did not agree with the decision not to publish the original article and consideration was being given to reversing the decision. I expressed to the special issue editors that I had accepted the original decision and that I wanted my editorial 'Talkin' Down to the Black Woman'[44] to stand in its place. I wanted the storytelling war that we are in to be on the public record and in real time. I would later come to learn that the managing editor, the editor-in-chief and several other board members of the *Australian Feminist Law Journal* were no longer *there*. By this point, I had also found a home for the story I was not permitted to tell.

It is here.

3

the unpublishable story

ISSN: 1320-0968
VOLUME 45
ISSUE 2
DECEMBER

did you forget whose land you're on?

Australian
Feminist
Law Journal

A CRITICAL LEGAL JOURNAL

Routledge
Taylor & Francis Group

I am interested in stories: both the stories that are told *about* us and the ones that are told *by* us. There is almost always a disjuncture between the two, and for much of my upbringing I thought that this disjuncture was a product of the illegitimacy of my identity, rather than a misrepresentation of my reality. I could never be quite Black enough, bad enough, sad enough or ancient enough to be like the Blackfullas in the texts I had encountered. I do not subscribe to the 'naïve belief' that Marcia Langton critiques, which presupposes that 'Aboriginal people will make "better" representations of us' simply because we are Aboriginal;[1] rather, as Jeanine Leane notes, 'Black writing has interrupted the unquestioned privilege of whites to represent non-whites in Australia.'[2]

The stories produced about us, and occasionally for us, are often unrecognisable to us in describing our being in the world, yet they remain tragically familiar to us as oppressive instruments that inform social policy and regulate even the most mundane daily encounters, from which we cannot escape. These narratives tell us less about Aboriginal people, and more about the parameters within which we are permitted to exist in the 'settler consciousness'[3] – and I speak not just of fictional texts, but of any number of scientific research reports. Thus, reclaiming what is ours involves reclaiming who we are and denouncing what we are not, and it is at the site of the story that such work must be undertaken.

Aboriginal writer Alexis Wright describes this 'storytelling war', acknowledging the difficulty facing Aboriginal people in telling stories beyond that which we have been conditioned to tell.[4] The revision of story is not a proclamation of good stories in favour of bad stories, nor is it an issue of ancient and authentic ones. Rather, what demands our attention is the task of revealing the purpose that these fictions serve. Both Wright and Leane associate the regulation and control of Aboriginal stories with the enablement and extension of colonial control over Aboriginal lives and lands.[5]

Indeed Chimamanda Ngozi Adichie in her TED Talk infamously quoted the Palestinian poet Mourid Barghouti who claimed 'if you want to dispossess a people, the simplest way to do it is to tell their story and to start with "secondly"'.[6] She cautions of the power and the danger of the single story, not as untrue but as incomplete.[7] Despite its incompleteness it frequently takes hold as the only story and thus the only truth that can be known about a particular people. Such stories emphasise difference, rob people of their dignity and make 'our recognition of our equal humanity difficult'.[8]

finding eliza

Several years ago, I heard Distinguished Professor Larissa Behrendt tell the Eliza Fraser[9] story, which included the so-called cannibals of Fraser Island, or K'gari, as it is known by the

Butchulla. She was speaking to a largely Indigenous audience, and I remember hanging off her every word as she narrated the story of both the Indigenous and non-Indigenous characters within the Eliza Fraser shipwreck tale. It was like watching a really good movie – we could actually see ourselves, because in her revised narration we were not savages but humans, and in fact heroes who saved Eliza Fraser from a likely death.

It was a more complete telling of the story that contrasted significantly with 'the drama of the white woman among savages' narrative that Behrendt had first encountered when she read Sarah Carter's *Capturing Women: The manipulation of cultural imagery in Canada's Prairie West* in a bookshop in Saskatoon some years earlier. In 2016, Behrendt's book *Finding Eliza: Power and colonial storytelling* was published by University of Queensland Press (UQP).

Behrendt observed that in the various accounts about Aboriginal people, whether told by Eliza or others, the Aboriginal characters were not 'well-rounded'.[10] The Butchulla are an unnamed 'shadowy threat; too savage to be characters, personalities or people'.[11] Their presence, she stated, was 'a canvas against which to explore Ellen's[12] psychological journey'.[13] In *Finding Eliza*, Behrendt interrogates the role that Aboriginal characters – both men and women – play in upholding Eliza as the epitome of white feminine virtue.

Fraser's femininity, according to Behrendt, 'gives her particular vulnerability and creates the spectre of sexual danger',[14] whereby she is constantly under threat from the nameless and barbaric Aboriginal men who desire her and the jealous Aboriginal women who envy her beauty.[15] Aboriginal women are depicted as the real villains in the story, portrayed as promiscuous, vindictive and bad mothers,[16] deemed far crueller and uglier in appearance than Aboriginal men and devoid of 'domestic skill or maternal instinct'.[17]

There was also the prospect of cannibalism among the Aboriginal people in the Eliza Fraser story, which Behrendt points out is present in most 'captivity narratives from the United States, Canada and the Pacific'.[18] This constant impending danger ensured a more compelling plot but, according to Behrendt, it also served a political purpose. In colonial literature white women are represented as 'objects of purity, symbols of domesticity, moral standard bearers of their race and class'.[19]

The juxtaposition of the savagery of the Aboriginal people is thus more pronounced and is a necessary narrative for justifying the need to take control of Aboriginal lives and land. Aboriginal people are not sophisticated enough to have property laws and consequently the land is for the taking.[20] In Eliza's first encounter with the Butchulla, she describes them as 'frightful looking savages approaching us, apparently with the ferocity of wild beasts'.[21] She goes on to state 'they were extremely filthy, never cleansing themselves with water ... their habitations but miserable hovels, fit only for those whose customs and habits degrade them to the level of young beasts'.[22]

Behrendt notes that Aboriginal savagery in colonial literature also helped mask the brutality of colonisation upon Aboriginal people. During the time of Eliza Fraser's sordid tale of captivity at the hands of the Butchulla, the genuine captivity stories were those of Aboriginal women being abducted, murdered and sexually abused and exploited by white men on the frontier.

Eliza's story of 'native savagery' also serves a personal political purpose, with Behrendt highlighting how Fraser exaggerated the savagery of the Butchulla to profit from her story. Behrendt contests the 'damsel in distress' narrative, noting that Fraser survived the shipwreck when all other companions perished. Fraser goes on to remarry in secret while peddling an embellished story of 'native savagery' for financial gain. Interestingly Behrendt offers a somewhat sympathetic analysis of Eliza, conceding that she did not necessarily have control of her own story once it was in the hands of others. She notes that the Eliza Fraser story is an example of colonial literature and a product of its time. But if Eliza's tale of captivity is of its time, we must ask ourselves: what time are we in right now?

finding caffey

In the very same year *Finding Eliza* was published, UQP also published a book by another lawyer, a non-Indigenous woman named Cathy McLennan, titled *Saltwater: An epic fight for justice in the tropics*. And that's where the similarities end. Well, at least between the authors/lawyers McLennan and Behrendt. It is the similarities between Cathy and Eliza, the white female protagonists, that are most fascinating.

McLennan, according to her own account, 'didn't have

much money' growing up, working in her family's small resort on Magnetic Island in north Queensland.[23] It was not fancy, but as it turns out it did attract some famous legal professionals, including Justices and Queen's Counsels.[24] Some twenty years ago when she first became a barrister, McLennan landed a job working for the Aboriginal and Islander Legal Service in Townsville,[25] or what she refers to as 'the tropics'.[26] The tropics do sound more exotic than Townsville and far more perilous for a white woman than the family resort she grew up on just thirteen kilometres away.

McLennan worked for the Townsville Aboriginal and Islander Legal Service for two years around two decades ago, but her experiences and her memories are deemed sufficient to provide the material for her first book, which is also touted as a memoir.[27] And sure enough, one of her literary inspirations is Paula Shaw's *Seven Seasons in Aurukun: My unforgettable time at a remote Aboriginal school*.[28] Like McLennan, Shaw spent two years in an Aboriginal community and went on to write what Greg Vass describes as 'an entertaining description of the exotic'.[29] In his review of *Seven Seasons*, he explains:

> Shaw (and the reader) always held on to the safety of knowing that she was only ever looking into the community from the outside, that it was by choice, and that she could leave when she wanted. Ultimately she was successful in presenting to the reader some of the issues encountered by a non-Indigenous person working in such a setting. However, her uncritical self-awareness in the construction of a representation of the *Remote*

was an ongoing concern for me … *Seven Seasons* told me more about Shaw and the socio-political culture that she comes from, than the remote Indigenous community represented through her prose.

McLennan appears to write in the same tradition as Shaw in drawing upon her two years working at the Townsville Aboriginal and Islander Legal Service. McLennan, in describing her book, insists that it is 'based upon real events, real crimes, real people and real court cases'.[30] She frames herself as the wide-eyed, fresh-faced beauty battling away in the harsh and violent tropics in what she says is 'the most terrifying job'.[31] Her distrust of and disdain for the Townsville Aboriginal and Islander Legal Service is apparent in the text. For instance, the reader is introduced to CEO Wally Greengrass, an apparently corrupt figure, by way of his large office, his ability to take the work car home, and his open-necked shirts which reveal a hairy black chest and gold chains. We are told about how he frequents the casino and boasts about buying himself a new gold bracelet with a bonus that he awarded himself.

The reader is also informed that the Legal Service's Palm Island office is used to store alcohol, and even one of the more trustworthy colleagues, she hints, is complicit in sly grogging on Palm Island. The final sentence at the end of the book in her 'note from the author' advises that, 'The Townsville and Districts Aboriginal and Torres Strait Islanders Corporation for Legal Aid Services, my employer at the time, has since gone into liquidation and been deregistered.'[32]

In McLennan's 'epic fight for justice in the tropics' there is no suggestion that the Aboriginal population are cannibals, though it appears from her account that they have very little care for each other, even their young. Almost all Aboriginal characters we meet are criminals – men, women and children. The central focus of this 'fight for justice' story involving Aboriginal people on Palm Island is the murder of a white man at the hands of four Aboriginal children, which is odd given the injustices Palm Island residents had been experiencing at the time McLennan was writing this book.[33]

Further, there does not appear to be any real interrogation of what an older white man might be doing associating with young Aboriginal boys by driving them around in his vehicle at night while under the influence and supplying them with alcohol. The scene is set: the real danger and moral outrage is configured around the narrative of the youngest person to have ever faced a murder charge in the state of Queensland (i.e. a thirteen-year-old Aboriginal boy), an innocent and helpless white male victim, and a white heroine, named Cathy, or 'Caffey', as the locals apparently call her.[34]

We know that Caffey is the heroine because Chapter 1 introduces us to her virtuosity as a child encountering the 'black bodies' that are the children on Palm Island some ten years earlier.[35] Her school on Magnetic Island took a Year 7 field trip to Palm Island by charter plane and here they met their 'pen friends'.[36] Caffey had gone so far as to save up to buy a present for her friend, with whom it turns out she's so close they call each other 'sister'.[37] They are expecting a big greeting upon their arrival, perhaps a banner even. But as it turns out, no-one is waiting eagerly at the tarmac to greet them and they find themselves walking to the school, only to encounter an empty classroom and some children graffitiing on a wall.

They venture down to the jetty for a swim and it is then that Caffey first notices

little dark faces peering at us from the bushes at the edge of the beach. Creeping forward. Slowly but surely our pen friends appear. Shyly glancing from under long, black, lowered lashes … Gradually one by one they join us … On that magical afternoon, we hold hands as we sail through the air … White bodies and black bodies alike glisten with saltwater. No words, only laughter. At that moment, for that brief time, two worlds become one.[38]

We never find out whether Caffey reunites with her 'sister' when she goes to Palm Island ten years later working for the Aboriginal and Islander Legal Service. Instead our first introduction to Aboriginal characters are Roslyn, her 'assistant';[39] Billy, who assaulted his girlfriend and has 'brown, discoloured teeth';[40] 'two dark forms' who run through the rain;[41] a lone nameless Aboriginal male in a prison cell who smells of alcohol-induced vomit and is facing attempted murder;[42] and a 'tiny girl' with 'greasy black ringlets' and 'large brown eyes' that are 'dull, without hope' and 'lifeless'.[43] Her name is Olivia and she is eleven years old and also detained in custody.

Olivia is a key character who reappears throughout the story and each time is fairly insistent that she wishes for Caffey to take her in and raise her as her own. Caffey writes, "'I wanna stay wif Caffey,' Olivia screams and for a brief moment I picture what it would be like to have her in my studio apartment on The Strand. I could keep her safe. But how could I get to work each day?'[44] Caffey, we are reminded, is the only one who appears to care for the children.

Yet we are also reminded that the Aboriginal children do not possess the innocence we usually associate with them. Rather, they are animals, and some children, we are told, lust after her. For instance, upon first meeting 'six bright-eyed, dark-skinned children' about to appear in Children's Court, Caffey claims that all eyes are on her, with one exclaiming, 'Eh, hubba hubba'.[45] Malachi, a sixteen-year-old boy and one of the accused murderers, has 'cold', 'deep-set eyes under thick black eyebrows',[46] which are 'snake-like' and predatory. As Malachi stares at her through his 'narrowed slits', she has a flashback to bushwalking on Magnetic Island and encountering a snake who was about to strike its fangs into her.[47] She writes:

As Malachi Butler's eyes bore into mine, I recognise that snake-eye look and feel the same thrill of fear. I keep still and hold his gaze. Then he shakes his head, his curls jostle against each other and the impression vanishes. Now there's only a vulnerable sixteen-year-old boy ...

Malachi grabs my arm, his eyes meet mine. 'We never done it, Miss. You have ta do somethin',' he says. 'We're innocent.'

'I'll try.' Heart thumping, I force myself to return his gaze, to remember he's only a kid, despite the chill that's brought goosebumps to my arms and legs.[48]

Malachi, a sixteen-year-old boy facing a murder charge, is subjected to several animalistic references from his defence lawyer, Caffey. Upon meeting him she muses that 'he'd make a good baddie in a film' because his looks are 'slightly off' and 'unusual'.[49] The other Aboriginal children, we are told, are Malachi's prey whom he pursues 'like a snake'.[50] It would appear that Caffey, despite her care for the Aboriginal children, has little sympathy for Malachi, even while employed as his defence lawyer. She writes:

'You did it. You murdered that poor, drunken loser. You know it and I know it. But I'm your lawyer and my job is to defend you. If you want to plead not guilty, then fine. I'll find you a new lawyer, a good lawyer who'll run your case and run it hard ... But don't lie to me and put on a show like I'm some sort of idiot ... You bashed a man's brains in, for nothing. For no reason at all other than boredom or pique.'

It's a calm and calculated rage that makes me use the word pique to make him feel small because I know it's a word he won't understand.[51]

Malachi is accused by Caffey of crying crocodile tears as a 'boy who is nothing but a crocodile inside'.[52] Malachi rarely walks; instead he lunges. In fact Aboriginal men tend to lunge;[53]

some characters lurch,[54] while others lope[55] and some 'trot' with their 'body flopping over stick legs'.[56] Charlie, a schizophrenic client who lusts after Caffey and holds her captive in her office, is described as a 'caged lion'.[57] He also exits a room with 'the restrained lope of a tiger'[58] and, McLennan writes, 'the raw energy of his walk remind[s] me again of a caged tiger'.[59] Joanne, a client seeking help, has a 'bird skeleton' hand,[60] while young Olivia has 'dark', 'scaly hands'.[61]

Explicit animalistic characteristics are also coupled with other dehumanising physical descriptions, which read much like Patrick White's 'animal-like' depictions of Aboriginal characters in his reimagined Eliza Fraser story, *A Fringe of Leaves*.[62] For instance, an Elder who proffers Caffey a compliment is described as having a nose like a 'prize-winning root vegetable'.[63] Descriptions of the physical characteristics of Aboriginal people within the text do little to tell us what they actually look like; instead they are deployed to evoke an uneasy emotive response at the presence of Aboriginal subjects or, as Leane points out, to represent the 'bonafide savage'.[64]

The eyes of Aboriginal people feature prominently in McLennan's text and are 'red',[65] 'dull',[66] 'cold',[67] 'weird',[68] 'scary',[69] 'busy',[70] 'bulging',[71] 'sad',[72] 'blank',[73] 'large',[74] 'deep set',[75] 'narrow',[76] 'beady',[77] 'without hope',[78] 'wild',[79] 'lifeless',[80] 'bewildered',[81] 'terrified',[82] 'frightened',[83] 'downcast',[84] 'exhausted',[85] 'desperate'[86] or 'full of despair',[87] 'dark',[88] 'puffy',[89] 'full of tears',[90] 'teary',[91] 'pleading',[92] 'confused',[93] fixed,[94] 'rheumy',[95] 'glassy',[96] 'hard',[97] 'empty',[98] 'dazed',[99] 'strange',[100] glaring,[101] 'staring',[102] 'animated',[103] 'crazy'[104] and 'vacant'.[105] Aboriginal eyes are like those 'from a car crash',[106] 'not registering',[107] 'beseeching',[108] widened,[109] 'flickering',[110] 'unfocused',[111] darting,[112] 'veiled',[113] burning,[114] 'glowing'[115] and/or 'glittering'[116] with rage, 'full of fear',[117] filled with a 'malevolent gleam'[118] and occasionally, twinkling with a spark of emotion,[119] they lock on her.[120] One of the boy's eyes are suggestive of brain damage.[121] The colour of Aboriginal eyes ranges from 'yellow',[122] to 'bright yellow',[123] to 'bluish',[124] to 'red-rimmed',[125] 'bloodshot'[126] and 'zigzagged [or] crisscrossed with red',[127] to a 'faded yellowish tinge',[128] while others look like 'chocolate-drops'.[129]

Complementing descriptions of Aboriginal eyes is the juxtaposition between *their* hair and *her* hair. Aboriginal hair 'hangs',[130] is 'limp',[131] 'greasy',[132] 'dirty',[133] 'all over the place',[134] 'matted'[135] and 'untidy'.[136] Her hair, we are told, is 'pretty'.[137] Caffey tells us about 'tuck[ing] a lock of hair behind my ear'[138] mid court case and 'nervously twist[ing] a lock of hair around my index finger'.[139] She pulls her 'wet hair back with a clip'.[140] As she arrives at the watch house to meet her murderous defendants, she writes, 'I sigh and untie my hair, still damp from my early bath. It falls in a heavy, knotted mass down my back. It's hopelessly tangled so I twist it into a bun.'[141] The 'warm breeze ruffles her hair',[142] the 'hot wind whips her hair'[143] and she 'runs her fingers through' it.[144]

Much like Eliza claims, Caffey – we are told by Caffey – is desired and lusted after by the Aboriginal male characters, old and young. She refers to the threatening demeanour of an array of Aboriginal men, including Charlie the schizophrenic

95

Aboriginal man who holds her 'captive'. Amid the murder case Caffey manages to find love with a reporter from the *Townsville Bulletin*, a white man who they both jokingly refer to as her 'personal hunter and gatherer'.[145]

Again, like Eliza's story, Aboriginal women do not fare much better. Aboriginal women are described as 'howling',[146] 'docile'[147] and 'quiet'.[148] Underage girls are promiscuous and grown women are bad mothers. The only good role for Black women is that of mammy[149] – the 'plump'[150] women with 'sweet',[151] 'goodhumoured'[152] faces and 'perfect[ly] round'[153] 'afros'.[154] They have a 'large'[155] or 'enormous'[156] frame, making navigating doorframes a constant struggle[157] and the furniture they are 'crushed into',[158] we are told, 'creaks'[159] underneath them. They wear 'flowery'[160] 'nylon'[161] 'tent[like]'[162] 'muu-muus'[163] and they 'wail'[164] and 'grunt'.[165] They are bumbling and dutiful.[166]

At the end of the book, Malachi confesses to the murder charge, while the other Aboriginal children are sentenced for lesser charges of car theft and manslaughter. The reader is left with a sense that there are few if any Aboriginal people who are good or whole, capable of being known as anything more than criminals, animals, or victims. The reader is left feeling helpless, but not Caffey, who in her final words writes:

> I saw Malachi as the worst of the worst. The true incarnation of evil. He knew no limits, no mercy. But in the end he fell on his sword to save his friend. Perhaps, if there's a pathway to redemption, he's on it. And for the first time in months, I feel hope.[167]

secondly

For Larissa Behrendt in *Finding Eliza* the reader is offered a more hopeful 'secondly' moment with the 2014 granting of Native Title to the Butchulla over K'gari. She notes that this legal decision represents a future that was beyond Eliza Fraser's wildest imaginations, but '*here* it is' Behrendt declares.[168]

If this is *here* it is hard to fathom how in the same year that *Finding Eliza* was published by UQP, so too was *Saltwater,* and it was the incarceration of an Aboriginal young person and the liquidation of the service funded to defend him that provided an apparently hopeful 'secondly' moment for *Saltwater*'s author. In her 'note from the author', McLennan thanks the judge who sentenced the four Aboriginal boys for reviewing her manuscript.[169] One would have thought the 2016 Palm Island racial discrimination case against the Queensland police and Queensland government would have provided a more poignant and optimistic 'secondly' moment. The failure to mention the death of Mulrunji in police custody – after having been detained over a petty public nuisance charge – despite it happening in the same place that *Saltwater* was set is a notable silence.

Like Eliza, McLennan uses her captivity story of life in the tropics among 'the Aborigines' to go on the speaking circuit, this time at writers' festivals and universities. She is lauded in the media for her 'insights' into crime, justice and alcoholism in Aboriginal communities. She is not simply a writer: she is a knower, via this account of a group of murderous Aboriginal children. It is striking that despite its animalistic depictions of

Aboriginal people *Saltwater* has been so routinely celebrated. This speaks not to the quality of the text but rather to the continued popularity of the 'drama of white women among savages' narrative.

Behrendt claims 'stories like Eliza Fraser's, in the way Aboriginal people are constructed and the roles they play, reveal more about the motives of the person writing the story than the Aboriginal people in it'.[170] In *Saltwater*, McLennan reveals her imaginings of Aboriginal people, and she also discloses her intentions for telling her story. This book is about facts, she claims, despite some amendments, which she hopes will help 'politicians and community members' find real solutions.

In *Finding Eliza* Behrendt declares:

> Stories like Eliza Fraser's offered a justification for the treatment and dispossession of Aboriginal people ...[171]
>
> Stories like Eliza Fraser's, told to advance the colonial agenda, find their way into institutions, including legal systems. They are used to sanction the removal of Aboriginal people from their lands and Aboriginal children from their families. They are used to legalise the theft of Aboriginal lands and dictate the terms on which Aboriginal people can recover their rights.[172]

Indeed, the uptake of McLennan's book at the same time Palm Islanders were pursuing a class action against the state government and the Queensland Police Service for racial discrimination in the aftermath of the death of an Aboriginal man in custody is not coincidental. Colonial stories of

Aboriginal deviance have worked to sanction inherently racist and violent social policy measures upon Aboriginal people – they are more than the stuff of nightmares[173] or enthralling tales of good guys versus bad guys.

While we might marvel at the tragic coincidences of these two texts being published in the same year by the same publishing company, it is clear that Behrendt's work is not in vain. In fact, it is only through Behrendt's *Finding Eliza* that we are able to find 'Caffey' and evidence of a colonial literature that continues to produce one-dimensional racialised imaginings of Aboriginal people as cannibals, animals or criminals. It was Jackie Huggins who declared that 'Aboriginal writing is concerned with history, with precise knowledge of the history of Aboriginal existence, gleaned, if necessary, from white records, and prised out of white archives' by the Aboriginal writer.[174]

Both texts, by Behrendt and McLennan, remind us that this colonial literature, despite its long tradition of domination, is not a historical one. Blackfullas remain typecast in roles that provide the canvas for extolling the virtues of white women and colonising agendas. Alexis Wright points out that Aboriginal people are 'relegated to being the primary informer at best to the professional person who then argues the story on their behalf'.[175] We are left wondering how we might escape this role of servitude in the production of the stories told about us. Again, Huggins argues that despite the external difficulties confronting the Aboriginal writer, the advantage we have comes through the relationship that we have with our communities, in that 'Aboriginal writers have a sense of purpose, an urgent task on behalf of their community'.[176]

It is the Black writer who offers our only reprieve and, notably here, the Black female writer who in her theorising about colonial literature offers more than a 'better representation'[177] of us, at least in accordance with what truths we are permitted to tell or prise out of their hands. In our insistence upon more 'well-rounded' characters, Black female writers have continued to simultaneously deconstruct, demand and offer better stories. Moreton-Robinson refers to the 'tactical subjectivity' deployed by Indigenous female academics whereby 'one can present a seminal paper and perform according to the protocols of the white patriarchal academy while simultaneously challenging its episteme'.[178]

Yet the work of Aboriginal female writers will never be lauded in the same way as the Elizas, Caffeys and Whites of the literary world, whose texts, rather than calling into question the parameters by which we can exist in the 'settler consciousness', serve to soothe it. And despite not offering better stories or better representations of us, there appears to be no satisfying the appetite for these violent colonial accounts. Much like Aboriginal academic, writer and poet Jeanine Leane, I too am left wondering, 'Who are the real cannibals?'[179]

4

on racial violence, victims and victors

QUEENSLAND POLICE SERVICE
COURT BRIEF
(GENERAL)

Prosecutions Original	Prosecutions Copy	CRISP Data Entry	Station Copy
	X		
QB	JAB	DRUG	

Date of report: 15/07/2000
Station/Establishment: DALBY
Phone No: 46699222   Pager No.

Code: 0725   Pros. Index:
Term id:

CONJOINTLY CHARGED WITH	DEFENDANT 1
1	Surname **WATEGO**
2	First Name (s) Chelsea Joanne Ruth
3	Date of Birth: Age: 20

CHARGE(S) - (STATUTE, SECTION & FULL WORDING OF CHARGE(S))   Total No. Charges for Defendant: 1

1. VAG. GAM. OTHER OFF. ACT, 7(1)(c). OBSCENE LANGUAGE

That on the 15th day of July 2000 at Dalby in the Magistrates
Court District of Dalby in the State of Queensland one Chelsea
Joanne Ruth WATEGO in a public place namely Cunningham Street
Dalby used obscene language namely the words "That Senior
Sergeant, Peter BAILEY, that fucking cunt, I'm going to sue him"

Witnesses: 4 Court Delay: Reason:

Failed to Appear ☐ Warrant Issued ☐ Date:	Court: ☒ Magistrates ☐ Children's	Date of Appear. 14/08/2000	Plea
Prosecutor.	Place: DALBY		
SM:	Prosecutor:		
Remands:	Defence:		
	Magistrate/Justices:		

Objected to Bail: **No**	Affidavit of Objection to Bail Attached: **No**	Bail Granted ☐ **Yes**	Reporting Conditions

Result: Date Finalised:

Driver's Licence Disqualified: From: Period:

Property Disposed of	☐ Court Order ☐ Forfeit to Crown ☐ Returned to Owner ☐ Other:	Property Recovered $	0.00
On date: / /		Prop. Not Recovered $	0.00
Photographed **No**	Certificate Obtained **No**	Total Property $	0.00

Arresting Officer and Leave Details - Unavailability of police due to approved or intended leave/courses

Role	Rank	Initials	Surname	Reg. No.	Unavailability From/To
Arrest:					/ / / /

But think of this: those of us who arrive in an academy that was not shaped by or for us bring knowledges, as well as worlds, that otherwise would not be here. Think of this: how we learn about worlds when they do not accommodate us. Think of the kinds of experiences you have when you are not expected to be here. These experiences are a resource to generate knowledge.

Sara Ahmed[1]

My interest in race is not a matter of intellectual curiosity. I have no desire to possess the most sophisticated articulation of it. I am a Blackfulla with some things to say about it, for race has always had a place in my life, especially in my resistance against it. Some would say it's in our resistance that the most violence is perpetrated. Maybe.

When it comes to race, I don't consider myself to be as 'well-read' as some. I read race on the run, not to outrun it as such, but to try and make sense of this thing in those moments – those moments that are meant to confound, confuse, crush. I seek to understand race from the place in which it has weighed most heavily upon my body as well as those around me. I want to know how it works so that I can beat it. And when I say beat it, I don't mean transcend it. I don't come from the place of mountain tops, of rising above to overcome race. And look, at one time in my life I mistakenly believed that being ten times better or just being more positive, as directed by my father, would help me overcome it, but I now know that strategy was one that was necessary for breaking even rather than transcending. And, even then, there still wasn't a guarantee of entry into the places that they deemed us unworthy of occupying.

Having to be better at any and all things has not offered any sense of freedom or hope, respite or relief. It has been tiring, so tiring; some days it is too hard to even dare to dream, knowing there will always be a damn mountain to climb or hurdle to jump. Strangely I still cling to the idea that I can out-think this thing called race; that is effectively what I am doing in studying it. Maybe it is that idea that I can do something about it which enables me to survive in a place that is so intent on our demise. Maybe all critical race scholarship offers is the illusion of agency to those negatively racialised. I think I find myself situated in the kind of racial realism that Derrick Bell[2] speaks of, one which doesn't demand passivity or outperformance, including the performance of pretending race doesn't exist, either now or in some future time.

I am interested in understanding race via the experiences of those who have been negatively racialised here, and not via a literature from elsewhere. It is via the embodied knowledges of Blackfullas that there is so much to learn about race. We continue to theorise and strategise survival, not just as an ancient culture in an ancient land, but as a living one that has long navigated the violence of race in this place, every day, all the time. Our supposed failure to climb out of socioeconomic disadvantage is not evidence of a failed strategising around race, but instead illuminates the function of an Indigenous critical race theory, one which foregrounds sovereignty over equity. This distinction as a people who are both Black and Indigenous calls for an emancipatory critical race imagining of 'standing still' rather than 'progress' towards inclusion. As a Blackfulla I am interested in what critical race theory can offer us in terms of our right to *be*, rather than to be remedied. As a people, Blackfullas, even when included in the category of Black, have long been deemed the 'wrong kind of Black'[3] and, at times, experience critical race theory as a betrayal rather than as an emancipatory tool.

Most of the time race conversations here are moderated by a self-appointed coloniser. Even the colonisers of colour still turn to them and appeal to them for guidance about what to do on matters of race in this place. Others appoint themselves to speak about race and 'colour', seeking to erase our embodied understanding of Blackness as originating from here, in all of our varying shades of Black. They will speak of things like diversity and inclusion because, sadly, that's the endgame of their anti-racism work: to be included in the same colonial project that continues to visit racial violence upon us as Blackfullas. They can enact a Blackness that is visible, but also palatable, one whose presence never seeks to disrupt the foundations of the settler colonial project, but provides it with an alibi against the claims made by Blackfullas of its brutality.

You would think that if there was one thing Blackfullas could actually know about more than anyone else, it would be race and racial violence. You would think.

I remember early on in my academic teaching career, both in Indigenous health and Indigenous studies, being greeted with an orientation that included an insistence that 'we don't teach guilt here' alongside the office tour, staff swipe card and a new headshot photo. I remember agreeing almost matter-of-factly, because I taught truth, facts and evidence – not guilt. There appeared to be a weird kind of whispering about *those* Indigenous academics who came before us, who allegedly sent white kids running hysterically from lecture theatres having been traumatised by the angry Aboriginal educator.

I had never encountered such an educator, but there was this sense that they existed somewhere. So I went about my way, teaching facts, and providing tools of deconstruction and reflection. It would be a good decade or so later that I would meet students of those educators, who would talk fondly of those unforgettably transformative learning experiences; experiences they would lament were no longer available to students who, under the guise of a student-centred approach, get to be cast as the knower of all things on race and Indigeneity, especially when the educator is Indigenous.

Every semester I would encounter chastising by students who insisted they knew more about Indigenous health and Indigenous peoples and cultures than I. These were the same students who had yet to distinguish between Aboriginal, Indigenous and Torres Strait Islander, let alone capitalise them.

They were indignant about how my facts made them feel, even in being provided a fairly straightforward terminology guide to assist them with speaking about us appropriately.

For some reason my non-Indigenous colleagues would uniformly stand in solidarity with these students, taking up the claim that we accept substandard scholarship in relation to Indigenous content because of the 'student experience'. We, as Indigenous educators, were not to demand more of them, even when they didn't meet the assessment criteria. Yet these were the same colleagues who during examiners' meetings, or extension considerations, frequently showed careless disregard for student wellbeing and their unique circumstances.

It took me a while to realise that in teaching Indigenous anything I was meant to be teaching students to feel good about being a coloniser; that in my presence I was meant to be the site of absolution both for the institution and its students. Despite transcending our role in the academy as engraved objects carved into sandstone, to enter classrooms as educators we are still being called to accessorise white knowing and affirm white belonging.

In being told not to teach guilt, I was meant to speak of trauma and despair, our social decay and dysfunction, things I had spent a lifetime contesting. I was meant to teach them the ways that they could save us, to redeem their unsettled self via sanctioning their continued control over our lives. I was meant to teach us as *problems* and them as *solutions*, so they could graduate to write those damn books about us.

But despite living in the poorest community in Brisbane,

which is known for its apparent social dysfunction, I just couldn't tell that story, for the simple fact that I knew it not to be true. It was in my knowing as an Aboriginal woman that I was rendered a threat, because in knowing my truth, I refused to accept the task of teaching about myself as a problem. It did not matter my pedagogical approach or the evidence base of statistics and theories; the focus was on the feelings of colonisers rather than my teaching as a scholar.[4] And at this point in my career I wasn't even speaking of race explicitly as an oppressive structure.

I realised that what was being asked of me was to produce a racialised account of Indigeneity that enabled them to pity us, rather than respect us. To this day, my being as a scholar is seen as problematic and threatening only because I refuse to reproduce the racialised knowledges embedded in this place about us that continue to operate upon our bodies in the most violent of ways. It's quite the paradox for the Black scholar and the Blackfulla in that we must not speak of race, yet must only ever know ourselves as negatively racialised subjects. I refuse to be complicit in the violence perpetrated upon my body.

nothing but blue skies

I must admit, there was a time when I much preferred the idea of not thinking or talking about racism. It is after all, as Toni Morrison notes, a 'distraction'[5] from doing the things we are meant to be doing in this world.

I remember my first job after graduating from university

was as an Aboriginal health worker in a town called Dalby in south-west country Queensland. It was on the eve of the millennium and I was just nineteen years of age. I was constantly being distracted by racism. On my first day I was advised of how grateful I should be in having been appointed to the role of 'Operational Officer Level 3' as it was previously classified as level two, which was trainee level. The increase was in recognition of my university degree, yet I'm certain that the person who cleaned my office got paid more than me. I don't know what degree qualification the cleaner had to justify their position on the pay scale but I do know that health professionals who have degrees are typically situated in the Health Professional (HP) stream of the workforce. Yet here we were at the turn of the century and the only racially based health professional workforce in the Australian health system was situated among the cleaners; not even the administrative staff.

At that time, in that town itself, racism was of a real, overt kind. The 'don't go to the RSL; they don't like Blackfullas' kind, the using racial slurs freely in work-sponsored cultural awareness training kind, the police randomly yet routinely pulling you over and ripping your registration sticker off your windscreen kind, the refusing to rent you a house kind.

I learnt a lot about race and racism in Dalby, through its overtness in the town, and the performed politeness from the white nurses in my workplace. I remember how I stopped booking the work car for home visits and community meetings because it was just too tiring navigating the surveillance and patronising concerns about how and why I was booking a vehicle, which came from people who were not even my supervisors. Some weeks the cars would be all booked out for the week by Monday morning, and I couldn't help but feel it was to prohibit my access, as though they had a more rightful use to the work vehicle even though I was to cover a whole district on my own.

I'll never forget the time when the husband (my boyfriend at the time) had to kick the winning goal in a rugby league game against Goondiwindi. I remember this because it was one of those memorable race moments we have in our lives. It was a Sunday afternoon home game and, in a town that had but a few traffic lights, Sunday home games were an event. The club wasn't segregated, but in the stands there was a mob of Blackfullas who sat together. Certainly in the pig pen there was a little more mingling.

It had been a close game and it was getting near to full-time when Dalby went over for a try to equalise. The goal kick would put Dalby ahead by two; however, the try scorer had scored in the far corner. It was left to my husband to convert from the sideline, the same side as the stands and the pig pen.

Everyone was quiet, hanging on edge. I've watched him kick from the sideline countless times and I knew he could do it, but I was nervous. If there was ever a time to kick that goal it was that day. As he was lining up the kick for what seemed like an eternity, a lone voice came from the pig pen, 'White men can't jump; Black men can't kick!'

There was dead silence. I could feel the tension and I

wanted so much more for him to make the kick. He walked back to reposition the ball on the tee. My heart was thumping. Everybody was waiting anxiously. He got up and slowly took those long straight strides backwards from the base of the football. And then he retraced those same steps, slow and then faster to kiss the ball with his foot.

From the sound of the boot hitting that ball, I knew he'd struck it good. The ball seemed to linger too long in the air. It was heading in the right direction, but we all knew at any time it could veer off or fall short. We all sat silent as that ball swirled in the air. It wasn't until the touch judge raised the flags to confirm the conversion that we screamed, like proppa screamed, jumping up and down in the rickety wooden grandstands.

It wouldn't have mattered had Dalby not won, because Blackfullas won that day. I love when Blackfullas win, for the simple fact that we are never meant to win. The odds are always stacked against us to make sure we don't because the game is rigged by race. But I remember that win like it was yesterday and I have continued to chase it ever since.

It reminds me of the first try scored in the very first Indigenous All Stars rugby league game in 2010 when Wendell Sailor scored on the sideline. I was at that game on the very side he did it. It wasn't the try so much but the post-try celebration, where he pulled the corner post out and proceeded to mimic playing it like a didgeridoo while his Indigenous teammates did shake-a-leg around him. All the Blackfullas in the stand screamed and cried that day.

I still get goosebumps when I watch it again. It was the cheekiness in winning against the whitefullas but, too, what that act represented. The corner post represents the parameters within which the game can be played, and removing it, in that particular context of an Indigenous versus non-Indigenous rugby league match, was an assertion of a clear redefining of the game on distinctly Indigenous terms.

The winning was less about power over, but the power to be, on our terms, free from those damn indignities. Du Bois speaks of these moments as 'blue sky moments' where you beat them in a running race, beat them in an exam or 'beat their stringy heads'.[6] Those winning moments make it that little bit easier to breathe in a world that is intent on suffocating you, but the labour required to achieve those wins takes its toll too.

Fanon describes the effects of colonial violence upon the colonised as a kind of breathlessness, a breathing that is overserved, occupied, in what he calls 'combat breathing'.[7] Some days those wins feel like that gasp of air having had to hold one's breath for so long. It is a gasp of relief. Sometimes, if those wins are big enough or frequent enough, those breaths feel like pure exhilaration and joy, working to reclaim, redeem, or restore the world to how it should be, if only for a moment.

I remember when my husband returned to work the following day at his job with the local council, one of his workmates was surprisingly quiet. Turns out, it was his own workmate who had chosen that moment to tell the world that Black men couldn't kick, a Dalby local who in that brief outburst declared to the world whose side he really barracks for. My husband didn't say anything to him; he let him go, much like that moment after he converted.

You see, as we were screaming hysterically, he simply smiled in the direction of the pig pen raising his hand to point and wave to that lone voice. This was a stance not dissimilar to those made by other Black men to racist spectators when gracing sporting fields. I still remember seeing him jog calmly back to his position after the conversion, all the while his head held high. It was a stance I had seen at home too.

of black souls in black homes

This stance was the one I had witnessed my father take up: not so much one of winning but of a carrying on regardless, in spite of; one in which the violence of racism was a reflection upon them, not us. This wasn't a kind of race blindness soldiering on. We had a strong race consciousness in our home, and it was never one of victimhood, as people typically insist that it is.

Being aware of something's existence does not mean that we are automatically overwhelmed or defeated by it even in acknowledging the various ways in which it constrains our very being. It is via that consciousness that we are able to reject the violent logics contained within oppressive structures that seek to limit or erase our existence; for instance, rejecting the notion that we are poorer and sicker because Black people are somehow poorer morally, intellectually and biologically. I am keenly aware of the various ways in which these ideas continue to be inscribed upon our bodies without our consent, and I have to be conscious of them, so as to never let them in, to never let them find a home in my heart or my mind.

I think my father knew that it was only through our consciousness that we could be resilient to the violence of racism. We had what perhaps could be described as aligned with the Martin Luther King Jr camp rather than the Malcolm X anti-racism, which I know is a flawed and problematic binary. We grew up with the idea that racism was something we could withstand and outperform. We'd have to put our bodies on the line, but our revenge was to be in our excellence, never transcending, just chasing those blue-sky moments.

The images of firehoses levelled against Black children slammed against the wall of buildings in 1960s Birmingham, Alabama, speak to this kind of strategy, of always being better, rising above, turning the other cheek, a strategy of withstanding the brutality of racism as a means to transcend it. I know Black bodies to be strong, powerful and resilient but, damn, I wish they didn't have to be so all the time. You see, in the brutality of it all, those same bodies can sometimes forget the necessity and beauty of their vulnerability, and thus be deemed undeserving of protection, by whatever means necessary.

I grew up watching my father – who was born under the cloud of the Queensland Protection Act, before it was illegal in this country to discriminate on grounds of race – seek to withstand it each day. I saw the damage it did to his sense of dignity in the afternoons as he returned from work, having had his Blackness referenced in daily jokes about 'Abos' on the CB radio, being referenced as 'a stupid Black bastard' by his supposed workmates, being questioned about what special benefits he got because that is the only way a Black man could own a truck, and being made to wait last to load at the wharf because he once dared own two trucks instead of one.

These everyday encounters pale in comparison to what he experienced growing up, and what his parents experienced, but they accumulated, nonetheless. Yet the next morning I would watch him get up, whistling as he walked down the front stairs, his polystyrene esky in hand with his head held high, much the way my husband did after kicking that goal. That whistle was bright and reassuring for him and me.

Although, as a child, I was curious and sceptical about this optimism some days. I mean how does one whistle happily away to the daily onslaught of indignities? Maybe there wasn't a choice not to. I remember the feeling of racism as a child via these vivid sensory moments. I knew from the sound of the truck engine roaring up the road whether Dad had one of those days at work. It was always on the return home that we could *feel* the kind of day he had.

I remember the truck revving so loud we could hear it from miles away. We knew by those revs whether we should make sure everything was in its rightful place by the time he had crossed those four lanes of traffic to reverse that semitrailer into the yard. Some days we would hope that he would have the trailer on to lengthen the time to get the house in order. Other days we'd hope he didn't have the semitrailer attached because, if a day had been particularly bad, it could take an eternity to properly reverse it in the narrow driveway of our yard. It was a skill to reverse it in first go but, over the years, Mum and Dad abandoned having a fence on that side of the yard. I still smell the burn of the engine once that truck had reversed in the driveway alongside my bedroom window.

I can remember Dad's voice and that rare moment when it hit a pitch that extended beyond his usual range. It is hard for a child to witness her brave strong father have his dignity robbed. I still remember his eyes in those moments, almost haunted, in the same way they were when he announced his diagnosis of inoperable lung cancer. I guess racism is like a death sentence.

I know that look of powerlessness. I've seen it in so many others since. Hey, I've even seen it in the mirror. It is a most disorientating look. That realisation that no matter how smart, how successful, how affable, how palatable one is, there is no escape from that racialised location, there is no outperforming race. That feeling of powerlessness, the realisation that those moments of power we worked so damn hard to obtain, are just moments of the blue-sky kind that pass far more quickly than they arrive.

But when they don't come, we blink away the tears and we pull ourselves together. I remember the days when Dad would declare, 'I might be Black, but I'm not cabbage green', to those who tried to pull one over on him condescendingly. I feel those words often as a Black academic. But for the most part, I watched my dad get up each day as though every day was a new day.

'Turn the other cheek' was not just a euphemism from his evangelical Christian indoctrination; it was a life support machine. It was what the good lord instructed, but I'm not sure it's what the doctor ordered. In his forties my father was diagnosed with high blood pressure and cholesterol, and diabetes, and in his late fifties he was diagnosed with untreatable lung cancer and he passed away a few years later aged sixty-two. There really are some things that Black bodies cannot withstand.

As an adult, raising a family of my own, I saw those moments return in my home. I watched the daily indignities my husband suffered as a 'cosmetically apparent'[8] Aboriginal and South Sea Islander man working for fifteen years in the Queensland Police Service. He entered wanting to change the institution after witnessing me being arrested and detained in custody one evening as we walked home together in that little old town called Dalby.

That particular night we were apparently subject to a random street check, with the police later claiming that they were concerned for my safety as I was walking with a considerably larger Aboriginal man who they thought I was engaged in a dispute with. In Dalby, we were routinely stopped together and independently for trivial matters for which there was no charge, just to check if our car wasn't stolen, to check why we were pulling over to pick up a Blackfulla walking along the street, to check where we were headed upon leaving town.

But this night I got a charge. One swear word saw me arrested and detained in custody for several hours. They thought I said I was going to 'sue' a senior officer, but later accepted that I actually said I was going to 'see' him about my treatment. You see, I was on an Indigenous advisory panel with the local police to improve relationships with the Indigenous community and avoid situations such as the one I had found myself in.

Anyway, that night my husband sat out front pounding on the front door of the police station. We left Dalby when he got accepted into the police academy. On graduating he went to work in his own community of Inala, in the outer-western suburbs of Brisbane. His goal was to minimise state-sanctioned violence upon Blackfullas but instead he experienced its brutality and it worked upon his body and mind in the most perverse ways.[9] Our marriage of sixteen years lasted just one year longer than his service to that institution. Maybe that was a blue-sky moment?

While witnessing the dehumanising and emasculating effects of racism upon Black men in my home as a child and spouse, I remember the constant battle of trying not to entertain the logics that sustained it at our kitchen table. We knew race was not about us, but about the power white people wield without authority. Dad would insist that we were never to bow our head; we were never to submit to their authority. We were to hold our ground. In fact, my scholarly work today is a product of this racial socialisation. My parents knew that each day we left our home we would encounter a world that seeks to put us in a place – hierarchically, not in the relational way we know our place as Blackfullas. Knowing who we are and being proud of where come from, however, was the armour that we were given.

My dad knew the limitations of Blackness in its ability to remedy the injustice that Black people experience. For instance, the everyday school encounters and inferences about our capabilities by teachers would be met by him sending my white mother to go deal with 'them people'. He knew the indignant white woman would be far more effective in dealing with the white female teachers than he could be as a Black man.

I'm yet to accept that one, and I often forget my place in speaking up about racism. I find myself taking the stance modelled by my indignant white mother, forgetting that I will never be framed as a well-intentioned white woman. I am always that angry Black woman. But then again, it is not as though I had the choice my father did, to send a white parent to take up the case for my children. And besides, if there is one place I'm most happy to put my race scholarship to work, it is in the defence of my children who have had to carry its effects on their souls and in our home.

Choice really is a privilege when it comes to navigating race. I have learnt to rely heavily upon the idea of it, I think perhaps to afford me the illusion of agency, of possibilities even in my most disempowering moments. I have also had to be kinder to myself in the moments when I could see no choice, because some days – hey, most days – we might not have any.

I have seen mob beat themselves up for not making the better choice, saying 'I should've done this' and 'why didn't I?' The idea of choice while being a necessity can also be the stockwhip that we crack upon our own backs some days. I think I came to race professionally because I didn't want to have to operate in the same way my father did as a truck driver or the way my husband did as a police officer. I didn't want to get up each day having to pretend that race wasn't real while having to strategise around it every damn day. But I don't think I'm any freer as a result.

the price we pay

I feel compelled to speak of the realness of race and all its violence upon the bodies and souls of Blackfullas because for much of my life every time I stepped outside my house I was forced to accept the colonisers' claim of its unrealness, only to return home each day feeling its brutality and seeing the wounds it left. Even working in Indigenous health, attending to the racialised health outcomes we experience, I was forced to pretend race wasn't real. And it was in being silent about it that it was the most violent.

There are too many leading Indigenous health researchers who remain invested in avoiding race because it has been more profitable to speak of other things. One can get millions of dollars talking about the incapability of the Black body, so long as you don't speak of the real cause of contamination. And, man, have they built those empires, dressed up as excellence, that serve to brutalise Blackfullas.

My career in Indigenous health hasn't been particularly profitable because I couldn't stick to the script that those good doctors are writing, having known that what they offer isn't even providing symptomatic relief. Under the mentorship of Dr David Singh, I took up the study of race so I could work out a different strategy for surviving in this place.

When I speak of survival, I mean literally. My five children don't know a grandfather and their father some days wasn't recognisable. I would be lying if I said that it didn't rob them of a mother some days too. The price paid by Blackfullas in our varying strategising around race has been far too great a burden to bear, particularly for those following after us. I want to do work that makes it easier for our children to be, but not via lies meant to protect them.

I am still annoyed at my father some days. In the weeks before he died, he insisted that he be cremated rather than buried. He hated funerals, in particular watching children grieve for their parents at gravesites as they were laid to their final rest. He didn't want that suffering for us, so in some weird way he thought he was protecting us by not having us watch him go into the ground.

But in doing so, he denied us the right to mourn and grieve in the way that was most familiar to us, and for a good while our family struggled because we were at a loss for how to grieve and remember him. On anniversaries, father's days and birthdays, I would go to the rock where his ashes were laid, but I soon stopped going because he wasn't there. I think sometimes in our efforts to protect ourselves from the reality of things, we can do all kinds of untold damage.

To speak of race in this place is hard. We find ourselves no longer welcome in a whole host of spaces. I once had a home in health when I spoke about culture and strengths. But when I spoke of race in editorials, keynotes and international fora, I no longer had a home in my discipline or school. I received those defamation threats at my job, copied to my manager and the dean of my faculty.

When I write about my experiences of racism, it is me who has to remind the legal department of my right to academic freedom, collect the evidence and craft the response. When I joke about incidents of racism on campus on my radio show *Wild Black Women*, a representative from the institution will have a word with me; not to address the racism I encountered, but instead to insist I not talk about it. Those directives are never put in writing, but there is no question that I am meant to heed them. When I submit a peer-review journal article or book chapter in which I've been asked to write about my experiences of racism, there will always be an additional peer-review process before it goes for copyediting, and even then it might not get published.

And despite what some may say, there really is no pretty or palatable way to talk of race and racism. To speak of race must be to tell the truth of its brutality upon Black people in whatever medium or by whatever means necessary. There are no 'two-sides' balanced takes. There are victims and perpetrators, and to tell truthful stories of race means that good white folks will be cast in the role of villain, which will get you in trouble every damn time.

There was a time when I did think that there was a way to speak of race to the colonisers that would make a difference. I used to think we could take an educative approach to race, not via culture, but by understanding how race works. Inspired by the work of Stuart Hall in 'Teaching Race'[10] I thought deeply about attending to the emotional attachment to ideas of race intellectually in order to undermine it. But I soon found that there isn't even room to teach race or talk about race in this place. This absence of interest in race is not because they know not how race works; rather they know they can deploy it to make sure things stay just the way they are and they will go to any lengths to enforce it.

In any workplace or institution of the colony we can witness the Black worker going to great efforts to do the additional work of being the educator on any and all things Black, on top of the job they were employed to do. This multitasking takes its toll even on the best of us. Of course, there are always some who are all too happy to be the dutiful Black whisperer translating the habits of 'the natives' to the colonial institution that employs them, on the proviso they get regularly rewarded with promotions and advancements. They are the 'first of their tribe' kind of folks who, in being so focused on being the first, forget about the advancement of the rest.

For most of the Indigenous-identified workforce in colonial institutions who are the least paid but most qualified, in the least secure of employment but the hardest working, that 'educative approach' to race takes its toll eventually. And look, as someone who has case-managed many white colleagues in Black spaces throughout the course of my career, I have to tell you, they really can't be told. Even when we offer the most profound insights and compelling articulations of our oppression, the settlers typically aren't impressed by it anyway.

I came to this position through the compelling evidence

of my own experience, including experiences that I have not spoken publicly about. My silence about these particular events was because I was still processing and strategising my response to them. I too had thought that silence was a useful strategy of protection amid the battle I had taken up.

But my silence hasn't protected me in the course of seeking justice, rather it has prolonged a silent suffering of having to weather the claims made about me without recourse. That suffering came to reside in my home and found a place in my soul. Despite all that I know and have learnt, I took on the shame of what happened to me, of being the cause or at least having consented to the abuse. I too carried the shame of responsibility for the implications of my actions upon those around me. Why didn't I just make better choices?

the inescapability of race

On the eve of what would have been my seventeenth wedding anniversary, I attended a Black LGBTQI fundraiser with work colleagues as part of our unofficial end-of-year work event. It was a big night and a mob of us continued on to a nightclub in the Valley, a designated Safe Night Precinct, which turned out to be not so safe for me that night. I didn't get home until around 7:00 am the following morning, having been picked up by my husband outside the Brisbane City Watch House bearing bruises that had not been on my body the night before.

I say what would have been our seventeenth wedding anniversary because, while still legally married, we had separated six months earlier, our relationship having been damaged by the racial violence he encountered in the police service, which came home to take a seat at our kitchen table over several years. He had retired from the Queensland Police Service on medical grounds, with anxiety, depression and post-traumatic stress disorder after fifteen years of service, as a direct result of the everyday racism of his colleagues and the violence of the institution he worked so desperately trying to change.[11] In hindsight we learnt much from that experience, about not staying too long in violent spaces, of not trying to be superhuman, of not running one out, of not trying to withstand, outrun or outperform racism. It doesn't work.

But here we are some twenty years after Dalby and I'm locked up again, in circumstances not dissimilar to those that saw him enter the police service. It wasn't swearing this time. In Queensland we have a new charge of public nuisance, the same one that issued a death sentence to Mulrunji Doomadgee within six months of its introduction in the state of Queensland. Two decades on, again I found myself pleading guilty, this time to a public nuisance charge, and this time represented by a barrister and with CCTV footage available that proved it was an unknown white male who was the aggressor and had to be restrained by security staff.

Yet within twenty seconds of police arriving I was handcuffed and detained, on account of the security staff's testimony. The unknown white male can be seen throwing punches at the wall then shaking the hands of security staff and going on his way. I was put in a paddy wagon, despite my colleagues' attempts to reason with the officers who were assaulting me. I was taken into custody where I was assaulted during a search, and again on my release. I was refused access to Murri Watch despite my repeated requests for them to be called. The officers that night claimed they called Murri Watch, but a check of the call log revealed no such call was made. The officers in their statement claim that I was taken into custody because I was too intoxicated to leave with my friends, yet they failed to take me to the Diversionary Centre, for public intoxication-related offences.

My original charges, I would come to learn, were failure to leave a licensed premises (despite being outside and beyond the entrance) and obstructing police. I obtained all CCTV and body-cam footage which substantiates my claims, along with mobile phone footage of what I and those around me would define as excessive force being applied during my arrest. The one bit of footage I don't have, the most damning, is the watch-house footage, despite having requested that it be preserved, and several 'right to information' requests and appeals. The police advised that they were not legally required to retain the footage after six months, despite their undertaking to preserve it. It does make you wonder why they would dispose of footage that would have likely vindicated them.

I remember the morning of my seventeenth wedding anniversary so vividly. I remember my husband taking photos of the bruises on my body. I remember wondering whether they were big enough to warrant the brokenness I felt. I remember going for a shower only to discover more, and remembering those moments that made those marks, while feeling slightly reassured that my body, via those marks, would be the evidence required to substantiate the story I told about what had happened to it.

I also remember feeling angry at having my power taken from me. Surely the Queensland Police Service had already taken enough from our family. I know I wasn't at my best at four in the morning, I was charged up, and still to this day I find ways to blame myself for the abuse I experienced. There are times when I feel stupid for having let it affect me, as though I should have been able to withstand it. I mean I walked out alive, didn't I? I felt both responsible for the arrest and assault, and undeserving of the role of victim.

Oddly enough, this event had illuminated for me another kind of violence I had been subjected to that I had been blind to, partly I think because I didn't have the bruises to show for it. You see it was just a few months prior to this that I applied for the role of director within the Indigenous health research centre I was working in. I was the only Indigenous academic with a PhD employed in the centre and led all but one of the research grants it administered. Despite being a partial appointment of one day per week, having won a prestigious research grant, I led the bulk of the outputs they reported on each year in their annual reports.

The role of director had been filled by a white male with no expertise or track record in Indigenous health who was acting in a part-time capacity for over a year, so I didn't think it unreasonable for me to apply. I was editing global textbooks, speaking at international fora on plenary panels and delivering keynotes. I was working ridiculously long hours to fill in for the absence of the white male academics within the centre because of my commitment to the survival of my mob and the responsibility to staff placed under my supervision.

My family suffered. It was at this time that my husband and I separated, with me having nothing left to give when I returned home late each night. I thought if I just worked hard enough the institution would recognise the work that had been recognised by others, particularly after all we had been told about merit and their commitment to Indigenous capacity-building.

But I was unsuccessful and not one candidate was deemed suitable in the original recruitment process, so the male academic got to run the place for another year while they searched the country for someone to take the job I was deemed incapable of doing. I got the memo and moved my research to another faculty to get on with the job. I wasn't going to withstand or outperform it, unlike my husband, I told myself, because I wasn't staying there.

But I didn't escape anything because over a year later, all but one of the team who worked with me during that time no longer had a job at the institution; some quit, at least three others had contracts that ran out, and some were forced into voluntary redundancy. I felt responsible for their predicament because I hadn't realised how my work around race would affect those around me, and their families.

Some remain unemployed now. And here I was with a job, in another school, based in a rented office a few floors above it.

But I was grateful to have been given a workspace because it was an improvement upon the last. That office I shared with up to five other people was much smaller with no kitchen, printer, photocopier or phone. It did have rat traps set up underneath the splintered desk I sat at though.

I tell these stories not to claim the role of victim, but to show the workings in how I came to learn about race and its embodied consequences. Whether I am the drunken Aborigine on city streets or the associate professor at a sandstone university, race is inescapable and its violence is identical. It would take me some time to realise that the racial violence the Black police officer experienced in the workplace was identical to that experienced by the Black professor. I despise the vulnerability that racism creates in Black souls, of broken bones, broken hearts and broken homes from the overwhelming weight of those seemingly trivial indignities, yet the body itself, I found, refuses to ignore the violence, the ways in which our minds insist that we do.

I remember in the aftermath of these events still holding out hope that I had a home somewhere in the institution that had offered me a permanent appointment. I remember meeting with a member of the senior executive on multiple occasions, who appeared to offer hope but, from my perspective, showed no real support or interest in my growing body of work. I found myself hard-pressed to find any substantial investment from the institution for the multi-million-dollar research grant I had applied for, despite their stated commitments to a reconciliation action plan and the development of their first Indigenous research strategy.

I was in one of those meetings with a member of the executive when it dawned on me that I was a problem to be managed rather than a scholar to be valued. I realised mid meeting that regardless of how successful I had been, nothing would change. I was breathless for a moment; so much so, I couldn't speak, and my colleague was left to do the talking. I remember regathering myself and finishing the meeting. I walked away, absolutely defeated, with my colleague for drinks on campus. He reckons I had that haunted look he too had seen before.

But it was in that moment, having been backed into a corner, that I remembered who the fuck I was.

David Singh[12] refers to this as 'sovereign divergence', whereby 'a settler hegemony structured in dominance is ontologically impossible much less total'. He explains, citing Michael Mansell, 'we are the first people of this land. We have suffered every indignity ever meted out to a people. Yet our strength is our determination … our sovereign rights as a people remain intact. By virtue of those sovereign rights we are the sole decision-makers about what we need and will accept'.[13]

It was at my lowest that I knew I had to act. It was in that moment of reclaiming or, rather, remembering my power that the feeling of defeat was swept away. You see racism is violent psychologically. It is disorientating, precisely to dispossess. It works upon us to insist that we forget who we are, and where we come from. But I was reminded during this time by Aunty Lilla Watson of the importance of operating on our terms, because when we operate on theirs, we have already lost. When we operate on our own terms, we are reminded that we already know far more than them. Cathy Freeman in the documentary about her gold-medal-winning-Aboriginal-flag-running 400-metre race at the 2000 Commonwealth Games states: 'I feel like I'm being protected. My ancestors were the first people to walk on this land. It's a really powerful force. These other girls were always going to have to come up against, you know, my ancestors.'[14]

on our terms

I am frequently called upon by other Blackfullas, from anywhere and everywhere, for assistance in how to resist or respond to racism. Typically I am asked to provide them with the language (i.e. what to read) and evidence to help tackle a scenario which in their minds is centred around appealing to whiteness in all kinds of settings.

The advice I offer is what Aunty Lilla has offered me. I remind them that it is not about the evidence base or their articulation of race theory. The strategy is all in their being, in how they are turning up. Are they asking or are they demanding? But I also remind them that they alone are best capable of defending themselves and their loved ones and that they already know more than the people they are up against.

In every situation I have fought, it has always been me who has worked through the night, collecting the evidence, and drafting the narrative for my defence. I am the only one who believes that I am worth fighting for. And I know that I am the best fighter there is. I remind them not just of the need to fight, on their terms, but that there is no-one else better positioned to do what they have been called to do. Fighting, not transcending, racism demands that we never forget who the fuck we are.

I remember one of my children complaining at the dinner table about my latest 'conversations' with teaching staff at their school in which I made demands on their behalf. He shook his head and said somewhat jokingly and awkwardly, 'I bet they all know me at the school', to which I replied, 'No, they know me.' I know that later on when I am long gone, my children will remember that I fought for them. And that in my being, they learnt that they were worth fighting for. No matter how well-read they become, the teachings I have offered in my being as their mother will hold them in good stead to become the fighters that they too will need to be in their time, for those who are to follow.

I remember sister Murrawah Johnson explaining so desperately about why she was taking on the fight against the largest coalmine in the world being built on her country. She had been forced to pay a price for that fight, a fight that in all likelihood she would lose. She spoke of her ancestors as immediate and present, not as distant or past. She spoke of the stories of their long tradition of resistance, the stories she was raised on. I still remember her tearfully explaining, 'I don't want to be the broken link in the chain.' Black resistance isn't new, and the wins and the lessons are to be found in our turning up, in our being, all the time, everywhere, even on our worst days.

Fighting racism reminds me of the organised physical disputes that take place in our communities, when things have escalated to the point that this is the only way to resolve it.[15] What is most interesting about this traditional practice is it doesn't matter who wins or loses the fight; what matters is people turn up. They turn up to resolve the conflict, they turn up to witness the event, to adjudicate on it, so that we can return to living our lives coexisting in some form of peace.

Now, race, like any other conflict, isn't going anywhere anytime soon, or at all for that matter, so we must think about how we 'resolve' the conflict of race everywhere and all the time, and what learnings can be witnessed and shared each time we turn up. It cannot be via a white civility that muzzles Black testimony, Black pain or Black rage. It must be on our terms and it must include a public airing – after all, the witnesses play a most important role for the parties seeking settlement and justice. Secrecy almost always serves the perpetrators' interests rather than the victims, who often must watch on in silence as the unnamed perpetrators parade themselves to an unsuspecting public as caring and virtuous. I can testify to the experience of that violence too, not to mention the betrayal by Blackfullas who are only too happy to perform the lie for the rewards it offers them, knowing that they too have been protected by the institution and the silencing mechanisms it can enforce. But, in the context of the organised public fight, there is nowhere for anyone to hide, and it is in that public accountability, even as a process, that justice can at least be sampled if not fully obtained. And besides, there really is no force more powerful than a Black woman who has put her hair in a bun and her bike pants on.

I used to joke about being an anti anti-racist because so much of what is categorised as anti-racist scholarship and practice still refuses to acknowledge the knowledges of Blackfullas and in doing so actively sustains the power of race in its own processes. Anti-racist scholarship and practice is still monopolised by colonisers and colonisers of colour and is centred upon appeals to coloniser institutions. Such a strategy is a long way from Kwame Ture's call for an anti-racist strategising predicated on Black power.[16]

A more genuine anti-racist praxis in this place should foreground Black power via Indigenous sovereignty in embodying the ideologies of the 'burn it down' and 'I am not the problem' kind articulated by Tarneen Onus-Williams and Aunty Rosalie Kunoth-Monks.[17] It must be unashamedly fierce in its defence of Black people rather than centre itself around a politics of politeness reserved for those who are brutalising them. That is the true test of whether they actually care for Blackfullas, whether they care enough to deem us worth fighting for, including risking the loss of it all. Typically they don't, and that's why we have to.

Of course it is scary and overwhelming, but that is why we need to strategise better around a Black solidarity rather than being a better kind of Black. This is not to suggest that the war against race isn't everyone's responsibility; rather it is a reminder of our strength, not just individually but collectively. I make sure I go into rooms where there are Blackfullas planted if only to be a Black body in the room to look to when it feels hard to breathe or to be the one who will greet you when you are done, to carry you from that place when you have nothing left in the tank, the one to laugh with or cry with or just sit in silence with, because you don't have to explain or retell the violence that just happened to your body – those eyes reflect back to yours the haunting of powerlessness. But sometimes we need to see it, if only to know that we are not crazy, that we are not imagining this shit.

There is a beauty among Blackfullas that we have retained despite what we have suffered, an unbidding sense of solidarity. It shows in how we turn up for each other – even if we find it hard to turn up for ourselves. I remember the eve of a national conference I was convening, 'Moving beyond the Frontline', about the Indigenous health workforce. It was a rare event in that it was for Blackfullas primarily, including all speakers and most of the participants.

It was at a small pre-dinner event that I sat with Dr Kris Rallah-Baker, a Yuggera man and our first Indigenous ophthalmologist and traditional owner of the land we were meeting on. He had recounted to me privately the response he had received to an article he'd written of his experiences of racism within his training. The CEO of the college he had trained at authored a public rebuff that in my mind was nothing short of offensive and condescending in its dismissal of his account.

Rallah-Baker had suffered more than what is on the public record. I talked to him about speaking of his experience publicly given the agenda of the conference and discussed with him how we might support him to speak his truth the following day. We enacted a range of strategies to support him to speak to Indigenous health professionals about being Indigenous health professionals in an honest way. It was fitting that he was speaking such truths on his own land to our people.

What followed was a line-up of Blackfullas shaking his hand, hugging him, and thanking him, which was in stark contrast to how his profession reacted. I saw the strength it gave him and I felt the energy in that room in that moment. It was powerful.

Within days, Professor Gregory Phillips contacted me about harnessing that support publicly. We drew up a public letter to Rallah-Baker's college with over a hundred signatories, including peak Indigenous health bodies, senior Indigenous academics and health professionals, including those from overseas. This resulted in a public apology and a raft of other measures that Rallah-Baker had called for.[18] Now the original articles from Rallah-Baker and the CEO are no longer accessible online, but the story of Black solidarity and the power of Black collectives to mobilise and take private suffering to the public square for recourse lingers.[19]

It must be said, however: Blackfullas can't always rely on the public square for justice. We learn this from Nicky Winmar, whose lone act of holding his finger to his bare chest to declare he was 'black and proud' at an AFL game some twenty years ago was memorialised. In his reflection years later to the photographer who captured the image, he said, 'I really appreciate you've changed my life, but for me, I'm having to embrace possibly one of the worst days of my life over and over again.'[20] In the calls for Blackfullas to be strong individually and collectively, we cannot forget the centrality of care in the course of this action. Sadly there is little care for Blackfullas in anti-race scholarship, policy and practice.

There isn't anything caring about insisting that we put up with or withstand the violence we experience or be classier in our responses to it. In fact, ordinarily victims of abusive relationships are told to leave them, rather than withstand the abuse or perform their way out of it.

But for Blackfullas, there is no escape. This is our land and we are not leaving, and neither are the colonisers. We have to know the limitations of their laws that give a pretence of protection, in particular the Racial Discrimination Act. But we still also must use these laws, because power is not ceded. Change must be compelled. There is something sweet in using their laws against them, even as a blue-sky moment, while knowing at any time these wins can be readily dismissed by the state as it sees fit. As such, our success when it comes to fighting racism should never be measured against our ability to hold them accountable to their laws. Our success is in our turning up, in holding our ground.

Anti-racist scholarship must be of service to Blackfullas in this task, inasmuch as it must learn from Blackfullas' thinking around race. Critical race in the colony runs the risk of being the new anthropology, having built the discipline off the backs of Blacks while claiming to know our experience better than we ever possibly could. Here, Blackfullas get to occupy the subject position of having experience while others occupy the role of expert. We can testify but never theorise, we are told, or vice versa. As a Blackfulla who gets to think about, live *and* feel race, I am unable to separate them out from each other. But this is not just an experience of my body; it relates to the rules that govern Indigenous knowledge production, whereby we cannot know without articulating our relationship to that which we claim. What drives critical race work for Blackfullas, as Huggins noted for the Black writer,[21] is the relationship we have with our communities. As such the knowledges we produce as Black scholars attend in the first instance to their function for our own Black communities, rather than seeking to adhere to the disciplines that seek to discipline us. It is from this place that we are reminded of the significance of this scholarship and its purpose, the success of which must be measured by the people who it is meant to be of service to.

It must be emancipatory, not extractive. It shouldn't be a taking of others' experiences of racism to theorise and debate who has the best take. In its doing it must restore agency, dignity and power, including the power to re-narrate one's own experience whether as victim or victor. In its doing it must be committed to undoing the power of race. It cannot continue to reproduce passive and powerless victims, or talk about race in ways that are inaccessible to those who are raced. I'm not talking about talking down to mob. I know what it is to talk to the souls of Blackfullas about the violence that has been done to us, in a way that may be unfamiliar to their ears, but nonetheless restores and redeems and, importantly, incites both anger and action.

Critical race scholarship must be courageous; it must call shit out in a Kanye West kind of way, not Kardashian Kanye, but VMA Kanye, telling the truths that everyone knows yet is too afraid to speak, at the most inconvenient of times and in the most public kind of way. It must be courageous enough to be unpopular. The critical race scholar must not masquerade as a neutral observer or as a historian providing a retrospective take on anti-racist activism – it must pursue the doing, inasmuch as it claims to know. Right now, Black women in this place have been left to do too much of the labour, and surely critical race scholarship must care for the people most affected by race; care not simply as an emotional expression but in a real relational and responsible kind of way.

The power of critical race scholarship comes from the struggle that it was born out of and its worth should be measured by what it does for those in the struggle. It cannot continue to divorce itself from those experiences of the bodies that bear the brunt of this struggle. I credit critical race scholarship with my survival and my sanity, in finding a way of thinking and speaking about a violence which, for the most part, people insist we stay silent about because we are told it's not real, with or without the bruises on our bodies.

Finding a vocabulary for the violence of race is not a matter of language or literacy. It is in being affirmed and validated about the realness of race in our lives that it's most useful. I have seen the psychological bruises of racial violence on the souls of Blackfullas; a brokenness of interrogating one's ability to know oneself, of struggling to believe the body's experience of itself. Critical race theory's use is in what it says to the souls of Blackfullas; in particular, that we did not imagine it, we did not deserve it, nor are we responsible for it. It is in knowing this that we find our way to get up and fight.

the final word on fighting

It's why I now find myself in the Malcolm X of 'by any means necessary' camp; no longer wanting to put Black bodies on the line, at least not without armour and arsenal to fight back but also to protect those bodies, knowing it can only ever be a harm-minimisation strategy. My labour in race, intellectually and politically, is no longer spent on appealing to white people either to resist or charm. Instead I have chosen to invest my time speaking with Blackfullas about race and racism, not to build their understanding of it, but to be in conversation around how to strategise collectively to undermine its power.

I know what it is to speak to the souls of Blackfullas about race in ways that are restorative. The air is thick, the room is mostly silent, sometimes you feel the sounds of mm–mm, sometimes you can't make eye contact because you will see those haunted eyes that stop you from speaking. I have seen tears in those moments, sometimes because I've spoken to them of something their body has felt but that they hadn't been able to speak of. Sometimes you see those tears that aren't of sadness but are of the returning home kind, a returning to knowing oneself. Sometimes there are tears of laughter too because being able to laugh about the foolery of those who thought they could take you out is most joyous.

When I first started doing the *Wild Black Women* show with my co-host and sister Angelina Hurley, the complaints we got were from whitefullas objecting to our laughter so we laughed louder. Sometimes we even read the complaints out to the sound of violins, laughing so loud we would snort. Maybe that's what Dad was doing when he whistled to work each morning. It was a refusal to be robbed of his dignity and his joy each day.

As a Blackfulla and a supposed race scholar, I still have this stubborn curiosity about notions of justice and freedom, not as theories but as sensory moments. I want to know what they feel like in the morning; I want to know what they look like in the mirror; I want to taste them – I imagine they must taste so sweet. I have tested the Queensland Human Rights Commission process for complaining about racial discrimination, not because I believe it will offer justice, but because of that curiosity combined with a responsibility I have as a Blackfulla to better understand what it is to do the very thing we call others to do in fighting racism.

There's plenty of people who will tell you to be quiet about racism, even Blackfullas. They will tell you to turn the other cheek and rise above it. They will tell you what you are feeling isn't real, that you are imagining it or overreacting. But don't listen to them. The only people who can teach you anything about fighting racism are those who have fought racism. In fighting racism, I have been forced to reckon with some of the lies that are told in this place, not just the lie of race but the lies told to those who are negatively racialised. In among the requirement to be superhuman, I had to be reminded again what it means to be human. And to be human was to allow myself to occupy the dual role of victim and victor.

It was not until I fought back that I realised such a location was possible. You see, when my body stopped for several months in 2020 I felt like a victim in being broken and powerless. I hated that my body had betrayed me, that it refused to carry on, and I continued to coax it into action, one chapter at a time, while also being present for those who called upon my time. I could still function a bit, so I wasn't a victim, I thought. And I thought to not be a victim in that moment was a good thing. I was going to be a victor, all the time.

But I hadn't realised that it was my mistaken desire to 'win' that had in fact immobilised me. I had handed my sense of self-worth and wellbeing over to an obscure legal process, which I knew from the outset didn't have the capacity to see the racial violence that I felt I had experienced, even with the evidence base and the argument. But it was in the act of my narration of what happened to my body, my refusal to accept their account, that I was also a victor. I had remembered, like Aunty Lilla said, to operate on my terms. In recognising that, I also came to the realisation of the necessity of being a victim as well.

Throughout much of my work, I have long resisted being seen as a victim. I saw it as weakness and incapacity, not realising what I was denying myself, and other Black people for that matter. I mean there was a logic, that in the midst of the fight you don't want your opponent to know your weaknesses and vulnerability, and you certainly don't want them to know that the blow they just landed hurt. Yet this work of holding violent perpetrators accountable demands a laying bare of one's wounds.

I distinctly remember when I realised that to be a victim was to be human. I was in the chambers of a senior counsel who was representing me in a race discrimination case. It was our first meeting and I had travelled a long road of two years, lodging the complaint, attending multiple conciliations, rewording statements of contention and arguing for my account of things to be believed and defended. He came across as arrogant and abrupt but in a determined, on-my-side kind of way. There was no question he was on my side and at no point was I required to defend any of the choices that I made in relation to this case. And as I watched him and listened to his strategy for fighting for me, I started crying. It wasn't just tears but a breathless kind of sobbing. I was trying to laugh it off, chastising myself for crying, but I couldn't sit there in his chambers without crying and I struggled to breath. The tears would not stop despite my best efforts. As he sat there he pointed out that I hadn't told the story of impact in my account of things, and certainly not in the way that he was witnessing firsthand. As I left his office, I was directed to write that story.

As I was trying to regather myself in the lift I realised that I should've taken someone with me to the meeting. I couldn't find my car in the car park and I suddenly remembered I hadn't organised transport for one of my children from school. That afternoon I felt so helpless and powerless and vulnerable. I felt like a victim, and I remembered that I *was* a victim.

That evening I wrote my statement of impact and I just told the story of all the things that happened as a result of what had occurred. I felt the bruises again, I felt the force being applied, and I also had to come to terms with the effect that it had in my home, on my relationship with my husband and upon my children.

Yet here I was suddenly able to speak of it, and even I was believing my account of my body. The words spilt out and I cried. But the strange thing was, I didn't beat myself up for it, and in fact I felt better and I had this knowing that none of it was my fault, irrespective of those supposed choices I should've made. It was in the telling of my story, the full account of it even as victim, that I was able to get a clearer picture of power and of violence, or at least how to distinguish them from each other. In telling my story, I could see that their power was exercised through violent force, and what I felt was not powerlessness but a pain that had resulted from their violence. And while this pain was real, the notion of powerlessness was not. That powerlessness had come via the stories they had told about me, and without my full account of things, those lies existed uncontested. But they were never true.

This is the powerlessness of dispossession – to think that our account of things is not worthy of being told, because somehow we aren't worthy, as victims or victors. No doubt there are those who have greater power to do greater harm but, even in the most uneven fights, we are never powerless. And our power is not evidenced in the same way that theirs is; it is not predicated upon exercising violence over others, but in exercising sovereignty – ours. And that is exercised in the stories we tell of ourselves, stories that don't demand we narrate ourselves as having power over others by only having the roles of victim or victor, of winner or loser. Our power is found within; it is embodied and it is enacted, every day. It is in knowing one's own power, even – and especially – in those most violent encounters, that we are able to remember how powerful we really are.[22]

When I wrote my story that night, I felt a victory, or rather a sense of peace; not the one granted to me by their process (because that never comes), but the one I returned to myself, in having relinquished an existence based on winning or losing and remembering instead what it is to be fully human, to feel and to know oneself as someone who is not just worth fighting for, but worth caring for, and deserving of better than what was on offer.

It would be just a few months later that I would be promoted to the position of Professor of Indigenous Health at another academic institution.

5

ambiguously indigenous

5640078158

CONFIRMATION AND ACCEPTANCE OF
ABORIGINALITY OR TORRES STRAIT ISLANDER DESCENT

Name of Applicant: *CHELSEA J. WATEGO*

Address of the Applicant:

Confirmation and acceptence of Aboriginality must be passed at a formal meeting of the organisation and be signed by the Chairman and Secretary under the Common Seal of the organisation.

It is hereby confirmed that the above named is an Aboriginal person/of Torres Strait Islander descent*, identifies as an Aboriginal person/Torres Strait~~Islander*~~ and is accepted as such by the community in which he/she lives.

* Delete whichever is not applicable.

RECEIVED
C'WEALTH
27 FEB 1995

Resolution Number: _____4_____   Date of Meeting: *23 / 2 / 95*

Moved By:
(PLEASE PRINT NAME)

Seconded By:
(PLEASE PRINT NAME)

Signature:
　　　　(Chairman)

Seal)
(　　to be stamped here
Signature:
　　　　(Secretary)

(Organisations' Common

They desired Indianness, not Indians. Indeed, admitting the
existence of living Indians called vanishing ideology into question.
Likewise, the presence of real native people revealed serious cracks
in the idea that once could solidify a postrevolutionary national
identity by assigning troublesome aspects of the Revolution to a
commemorative Indian-American past ... Real Indian people
both had – and had not – disappeared.

Philip J Deloria[1]

There is a new and rapidly emerging tribe among 'the native population' of so-called Australia. They speak of an Indigenous ancestry while being unable to name their ancestors, or Indigenous cousins even.[2] Instead they talk of feelings of affinity and/or grainy black-and-white photographs of great-great-great-grandmothers who *may* have been. These pictures typically get unearthed during a time in their life when there is greater proximity to Indigenous bodies, often a time in their career when they once worked among 'the natives' from another place or having formed an intimate relationship with an Indigenous partner.

Those without photographs will whisper about whispers in the family about that great-great-great-grandparent who may have been one of those people, or the estranged dad's dad who may have been but refuses to acknowledge any Indigenous ancestry; others will mention a deathbed confession to a family member several generations back. Some claim they have had a DNA test which proves they are 'Aboriginal'. In the absence of tests, others tell stories of financial hardship or social dysfunction to authenticate their ancestry claims, even when that dysfunction relates to the white side of their family. That's the function of dysfunction, I guess; even when not owned exclusively by Blackfullas, it can be used to claim proximity to us, ironically via white racialised imaginings of Black inferiority. In the absence of relationships to Blackness, imagined or actual, others join or form Aboriginal Facebook groups to seek out other members of their tribe, and, man, are they forming tribes online and offline!

Despite these newfound claims of Blackness, many of these people have grown up thinking of themselves as white, or maybe slightly 'othered', and for much of their life benefitted from a social location where they were known and seen as anything but Aboriginal. For all their claims of a past proximity, these people typically don't have stories of being socialised as Aboriginal. They often attribute this to some unknown and unnamed Aborigines they encountered at some point in their life, who allegedly deemed them 'too white to be Black'. In almost every story of Aboriginal identity crisis, you can guarantee there is an Aboriginal character or characters who are framed as dysfunctional, angry, unwelcoming and violent, and to blame for their ongoing disconnection. Thus their identity crisis is seen not as a problem of their ancestry, ancestors or actions, but instead as the fault of those damn Aborigines, which ironically is the social group to which they are insisting they have membership.

The 'angry Aborigine' is invoked in order to avoid accountability to Indigenous peoples for not seeking to be in relationship with them, and there literally only needs to be one bad Black in such stories. These unsubstantiated claims go unquestioned because to question them would be framed as an 'attack' on their Aboriginality. Consequently, the racist ideology of the hostile and aggressive 'native' is perpetuated unchecked, and why would it need to be otherwise, as this has always been the colonisers' account of things.

As a fair-skinned Blackfulla I have to say it has primarily been whitefullas or non-Indigenous colonisers who have suggested I was 'too white to be Black' and it wasn't always based upon a reading of my skin colour. But members of this tribe often have a preoccupation with skin colour and 'identity'. I think perhaps it could be because many fit in the category of being 'white-coded'; that is, their body is read as white by those not familiar with their ancestry, and for much of their life was read as such.

But I find this problem is often most problematic among those white-coded mob who have spent the bulk of their time connected to white people and white institutions. Having only ever been surrounded by colonisers' dispossessing identity talk, members of this tribe spend much of their time speaking back to them with metaphors of coffee and tea. Such metaphors work to contest the supposed dilutability of racial blood talk;[3] however, they fail to address a core feature of Indigeneity as expressed by Indigenous peoples and that is connection to Indigenous peoples, cultures and country. These connections are not evidenced by the colour of anyone's skin, making all the energy devoted to such talk redundant. How could one's identity ever be affirmed by the people who are so deeply invested in erasing it and more, rather than the people who you claim a belonging to?

I still remember an Aboriginal woman describing Aboriginality to me as 'if you got no relationships you got nothing'.[4] In the absence of those relationships the ambiguously Indigenous invest much of their labour appealing to be seen by the colonisers as Indigenous, all the while remaining disconnected from the very bloodline that is supposedly the source of their Indigenousness.

You will find that when these newly identifying mob are greeted by actual Aboriginal people with the standard 'Who's your mob and where do you come from?' they will scream 'lateral violence' to all and sundry, as though a standard introduction is a violent interrogation upon their body. That they associate a relational greeting with the same violence as coloniser inquisitions of 'How much Aboriginal are you?' reveals exactly whose terms they are operating under.

You will note that they are typically more comfortable with being asked, 'What do you do?' because their articulation of their identity and self is bound up in the work they do, rather than in their being or belonging. There are so many ancestry Aborigines who have come to the Indigenous-identified positions/services to do their identity work. When I refer to the Indigenous-identified position, I'm not talking about the administrative trainee role, but rather the Indigenous program manager, team leader or CEO. Despite being a bub culturally, their proximity to whiteness jettisons them into these lucrative leadership roles.

It is not enough to discover a past Indigeneity and become Indigenous; they insist that they are leaders, elders, knowledge keepers, role models and saviours. They are the better kind of Black, which the rest of us apparently lack the ability to be. They take up Indigenous-identified positions to claim their newly found identity, wearing the job title like a damn kangaroo-skin cloak draped across their shoulders.

And if they aren't tattooing their skin with an Aboriginal flag they will get animals done that they've appointed totem status to; some discover their hidden artistic skills using those damn cotton buds, some learn to play the didgeridoo, some adorn themselves with emu-feather earrings, and occasionally smear their face with ochre and feathers on their forehead to make their public profile more 'Indigenous-like'. The colour and pattern are not located with anywhere in particular – those dots do the work in screaming, 'Look, an Aborigine!'

In this role of occupationally Indigenous, the services that they are meant to provide to actual Aborigines run secondary to their own need for identity affirmation every damn minute of the day. Just like the Indigenous 'anything', they've co-opted the term 'cultural safety' to literally mean their safety against being held accountable culturally by Aboriginal people. This is particularly tragic because, as such, Aboriginal people are again denied the services they need, and which they have fought hard for. But, alas, the Aborigine encounters them in counselling sessions, whereby the ancestry Aborigine spends much of their time seeking cultural credibility from the client rather than paying attention to their therapeutic needs; the Indigenous student is cast in the role of prop to the newly identifying teacher who has forgotten that her job is to teach students rather than extract their Blackness. The newly identifying Indigenous nurse who struggles to work in a specific Indigenous cultural context redefines culturally safe care in such a way that emphasises their safety over the provision of health care to Indigenous peoples presenting in the clinical encounter.

In such everyday encounters, we see ontologically the limitations of their newfound ancestry. There isn't an Aboriginal flag tattoo big enough to hide the western conceptualisation of self and racialised imaginings of Aboriginal people that they are operating under. I remember Uncle Shane Coghill making the claim via the following question: 'If you have never lived as an Aborigine, then how do you think like one?' Sadly there is little room to discuss the damage upon the lives of Blackfullas who at their most vulnerable have to encounter the violence of care providers whose only care is to their own identity project.

told us all the white man's ways[5]

I remember once tweeting that I would not entertain discussions on Indigenous cultural matters with ambiguously Indigenous accounts (i.e. anonymous accounts or those whose ancestry wasn't declared). Just as there are fake accounts on Twitter, there too are fake Aborigines whose identities are unknown but whose Indigenousness is made apparent via their ambiguously Indigenous bios and Twitter handles. Such accounts are typically not interrogated and, as such, anonymous Aborigines have licence to make all kinds of claims to which they are not held accountable.

My Twitter thread was met with a fairly hostile response from many who felt it was a direct attack on their Indigeneity. One who claimed to be speaking on behalf of the stolen generation (of which many of these mob tend to do) lectured me on colonial violence and claimed that to talk of newly identifying or ambiguously Indigenous peoples is to invoke a new form of blood-quantum talk. I was struck by the swiftness with which a conversation about cultural protocols could be co-opted by the newly identifying tribe and constructed as a form of racial violence perpetrated by Blackfullas, rather than the colonisers who constructed blood quantum to explain away the erasure of the Aborigine. I wasn't speaking of erasure via racial eugenics; I was speaking about the persistence of Aboriginal cultural protocols. But this misreading was a revelation yet again of the terms upon which these people operate.

To speak of cultural protocols is not to dilute or diminish an individual's Indigeneity but rather to respect and uphold our ways as Indigenous peoples more broadly in a manner that doesn't privilege the self over all other things. Culturally, there are so many limitations to my knowing but I know that doesn't make me less Indigenous. So it is telling that those among us who claim to have been stolen and have lost their culture and/ or any connections to their people then insist on being the arbiters of Aboriginal culture and included in any or all things.

It is knowing our place that seems to be an affront to those who don't know theirs, and this is why they are dangerous in their disconnect. They insist upon an Indigenousness that is divorced from community and country, which is precisely the form of Indigeneity the colonisers seek. In having known themselves as colonisers first, they too seek to locate themselves hierarchically rather than relationally with Blackfullas. For instance, despite my repeated reassurance to this tweeter that I wasn't denying them of identity, they persisted to project their identity issues upon me. The irony here is that members of this tribe frequently explain their lack of connection, either past or present, as 'through no fault of their own' but are happy to blame every other Blackfulla for how they feel about themselves.

For these mob, culture is often a competition, rather than a way of being that gives meaning to the world. For instance, for some reason this person during the conversation insisted we were 'equals'. They became enraged with me when I refused to accept the means by which they were engaging – seeking to position us hierarchically rather than relationally culturally. I made it clear that I had never met this person before and I did not know them or their mob to know how it was that we were to relate to each other. Upon communicating this to them, they referred to our ages, my alleged arrogance and my possession of a PhD, which according to them was how I supposedly came to be arrogant. It appeared this person was unable to think about a relationality that wasn't configured around power, imagined or otherwise. Sadly they refused to recognise the harm of this engagement, even after repeated appeals for them to stop. As they hadn't respected these boundaries, I blocked the account. They then took a screenshot of this, declaring, 'I wish I could count this as a win.'

But this isn't an unfamiliar experience for Blackfullas in the colony. We are fairly accustomed to white people and other colonisers seeking to put us in our supposed place. Often they can't deal with our presence because it so vastly contradicts the imaginary space they had reserved for us in their mind. Typically we are removed from the category of Aboriginal by being labelled 'exceptional' or 'not really' Aboriginal. But in this instance, this person used my PhD of all things as a weapon against me, as though having it was reflective of me being uppity, despite never invoking it in our conversation. It was a bit rich coming from someone who is on the public record claiming their work was exclusively for a white readership.

These contradictions are as prevalent as the complaints among them. I have encountered several of this tribe who seek out or receive an Indigenous scholarship or benefit from an Indigenous entry pathway with or without a confirmation of Aboriginality. When they receive the opportunity, they won't disclose publicly their Indigeneity and apparently there are all kinds of 'culturally safe' justifications for their refusal to do so. Typically they will claim it is because they don't know where they are from. But if they do not know where they are from or who they belong to, then how do they know themselves to be Indigenous?

I remember encountering many of these people in higher educational contexts as students seeking entry into a degree program, most commonly medicine or law. Some would be required to provide a confirmation of Aboriginality document to access particular supports or entry via their Indigenous ancestry. Some students would need assistance in the process of seeking confirmation. It is most telling when someone seeks a confirmation document but cannot tell a coherent story about how they came to believe they were Indigenous, especially in the absence of close or even distant relatives claiming the identity. We are told that their family lives a long way away or they don't have the time to connect back to community. I would typically encourage students to be in conversation with mob to rebuild those lost connections and relationships, only to be met with resistance because of an administrative urgency.

But once claimed administratively by white institutions, the need to be ontologically Indigenous is abandoned. From the medical students who get special entry but refuse to wear the Indigenous sash across the graduation stage, to the scholar who presents his work and makes no mention whatsoever of his Indigeneity in his presentation, to the student who is heralded as an Indigenous role model, but who similarly doesn't want to be known as an Indigenous professional because that is somehow belittling. Here we see the problem of an Indigeneity that is detached from land and people. It is instead constituted via disadvantage, and readily abandoned once the claim of disadvantage is no longer advantageous for them personally. These mob have no shame in taking the opportunity but suddenly are shame to be publicly associated with *being* Indigenous.

And yes, of course individuals who are free to choose how their body is read are free to choose when to identify; however, they must also recognise the privilege as well as accept the consequences of their non-identifying behaviour. The most ridiculous of all complaints from those who choose to live a private and personal Indigeneity, that they draw on for administrative purposes, is the claim of lateral violence when they are presumed or read to be non-Indigenous by actual Indigenous people.

Let me say this loudly and clearly: if you consciously choose not to identify yourself in your work, in that tutorial, in your bio and in your being, you cannot run to white people to complain that Black people attacked your identity for presuming that you are not Indigenous. And, honestly, to invoke cultural safety as something one deploys to appeal to white people and white institutions to attack Blackfullas who are adhering to cultural protocols is yet another form of racial violence. As Uncle Tiga Bayles would say, 'That may be your heritage, but this is my culture!' And certainly this notion of weaponising ancestry claims to avoid adherence to cultural protocols was not, I'm fairly certain, the kind of 'cultural safety' initially conceived by Irihapeti Ramsden.[6]

I am conscious that in entering into a conversation about

these people, I will get myself in all kinds of trouble, not least of which will be accusations of lateral violence. The purpose here is not to ridicule the phenomenon of people who discover Indigenous ancestry, but to demonstrate the function of these folk in the colony. For they serve a function, and that is why mob are enraged – it is not because we are jealous or dissatisfied with our lives.

I am also conscious that this conversation runs dangerously close to an assertion that Andrew Bolt is accused of, in terms of suggesting that Aboriginal people are only claiming Indigenous ancestry for material gain. The difference with Bolt is that he identified Aboriginal people who always knew and were known to be Aboriginal. And the problem with these mob is not a problem of Aboriginal people, knowledges or communities, but a problem of the colonial-settler project. Bolt also mistakenly presumed, like most colonisers, that the only reason for identifying with one's Indigenous ancestry was economic benefit, because he could not see any other value in being Indigenous.

We know by and large that Blackfullas are the poorest people in this country. As mentioned, I live in one of the poorest suburbs in Brisbane and the analysis of income levels in even our community shows that Blackfullas are still poorer than the rest of the poor people in our hood. Put simply, 'being' Indigenous doesn't offer a pathway out of poverty. But as Blackfullas we know there is tremendous social value in belonging to Black land, Black families and Black communities. Those that speak of an Indigenous ancestry that is disconnected from people and place don't understand such value and that is a real problem that we need to talk about.

and others taught them prejudice

In the absence of an Indigeneity formed in relationship with Indigenous peoples, we witness an Indigeneity that is performed. Such performances typically adhere to the scripts assigned by the coloniser, and that is why these performers are most revered by the coloniser and their institutions. Some incorporate racist Aboriginal caricatures in their life narrative, while others become them. Through them we must suffer performances of cultural caricatures of the political, dysfunctional and/or cultural Aborigine.

Some adorn themselves with ochre and language words, others with flag paraphernalia and protest movements, and others with past tales of woe. I say past tales, because they are modelling an Indigeneity come good, through the good graces of white patrons or the white parents who raised them. They represent an Indigeneity of the past, a past Blackness that has been remediated so as not to pose a threat or risk. There are also those among them who articulate an Indigeneity which is predicated upon resisting those racist stereotypes – that is, they exist only via what they claim not to be. They are 'not the stereotypical Aborigine', they proudly announce to the colonisers, while remaining oblivious to how deeply offensive such claims are to Blackfullas. But of course, they aren't stereotypical Aborigines because they aren't even Aboriginal.

In their positioning as Aboriginal, but not like the rest of 'them', they are situated hierarchically rather than relationally. And that hierarchy is based purely on a proximity to whiteness. The ambiguously Indigenous will take coloniser platitudes of Aboriginal exceptionalism at face value because they have not known Black excellence as an everyday embodied experience. They fail to see that the only exceptionalism is in their mediocrity for the role they've been assigned.

Enter the 'role model'. These aspirational Aborigines are the chosen ones, for the simple fact that in their mediocrity they fulfil the need of colonisers for 'natives' as 'capacity-building projects' rather than 'sovereign subjects'. The role model may have completed university or have been the first of their something in a coloniser institution. In entering such supposed exclusive white spaces, we are led to believe that their individual advancement is somehow emancipatory for the rest of the tribe.

Yet, ironically, their supposed success is framed as having little to nothing to do with their Indigeneity; their achievement is lauded as though it's extra special because they have somehow transcended the supposed shackles of Indigenousness. Little regard is given to what was traded for the seat at the table or, worse still, what didn't need to be traded.

Tragically, the role model typically hasn't done anything transformative within their community or changed the material conditions of Aboriginal people. They earn the title of role model because they have successfully navigated a coloniser institution without disrupting it. This success is only possible because the newly identifying ancestry Aborigine in their proximity to whiteness has not experienced difficulties navigating these institutions; after all, it has been part of their survival strategy up until this point.

But those who are ontologically Indigenous are simply unable to pretend that the violence of coloniser institutions isn't bearing down upon their bodies and souls. The ontologically Indigenous within coloniser institutions will disrupt the standard order of things in their being, will force rules to be reviewed, will be deemed noncompliant, at risk, and a problem. And this apparent deviance will be attributed to Black lack, rather than being recognised as Black will: the will to remember, the will to retain what it is to be Indigenous, in spite of all of their best efforts.

When colonisers talk of Indigenous role models, they are speaking of role models for the colonial-settler project, one whose goal remains to absorb Indigenous peoples into the general population, so that we ultimately forget that we were ever Indigenous. As role models, the ambiguously Indigenous will be cast in leadership and managerial roles for which they aren't equipped, but they will be most efficient in cracking the stockwhip over the rest of us.

You see this strategy isn't new. Native police were seen as a cost-effective way to quell Indigenous resistance with units established across the country from the early to mid 1800s to the early 1900s.[7] They were brought in from other regions so they had no accountability to local people and their function was purely punitive, to aid in colonial expansion and do away with 'natives' getting in the colonisers' way. Their violence, some argue, was unbridled yet sanctioned by the colonisers. Given the native police committed the deeds, the system worked to minimise reprisals against local colonisers too.

The role-model Aborigine works as the new native police in the colony, except rather than coming from elsewhere, these ones come from nowhere, and that can be evidenced in bios where bloodlines aren't declared. Rarely will you find coloniser institutions employing or instating role models who are traditional owners in leadership positions. In fact in some institutions you will see them actively removing traditional owners from any role at all, beyond the ceremonial function they are meant to serve. Traditional owners don't make for good role models, because in their knowing of who they are and where they come from they are the Black speed bumps hindering the ongoing colonial project. Thus the aspirational Aborigine from elsewhere is brought in to deal with 'the troublesome natives' in those new leadership positions.

The elsewhere Aborigine will infiltrate Indigenous spaces so they are no longer safe for actual Indigenous peoples. These spaces, however, are not the densely populated, materially poor Indigenous community, but instead the bustling Indigenous service-delivery context, whether the corporate sector, arts, academia, or government. It is in the business of Indigenous affairs that these ones find themselves in positions of power over Indigenous peoples.

And it is the ambiguously Indigenous who are most dispossessing in their deeds, undoing any sense of progress Blackfullas have achieved. They move into institutions to disperse 'the natives' who have formed Black collectives to regain some sense of power. They invoke the language of mainstreaming, which, much like dispersal, masks the violence inflicted upon Black people in breaking up long-established supportive cultural, political and intellectual communities.

These elsewhere Aborigines are more than willing to visit violence upon Blackfullas who are engaged in acts that serve Indigenous peoples and collectives exclusively. Such groups are seen as threatening to them because they are communities which they are not part of, and which refuse to credentialise them. But they will claim that it is they who are advancing our interests, about which we just don't know any better.

This role has value for them as they are rewarded nicely by those they are seeking approval from while dispossessing those who they are most envious of. In their trauma, and having not resolved their own identity, the ambiguous Aborigine visits the most violence upon those who refuse to acquiesce to them and sanction the governor-general role they have taken up for the colonial project. Rarely are these new native police seen as the violent perpetrators that they are. That executive coaching has taught them how to accessorise well.

The irony of this all is, it's the new native police who scream lateral violence in any and all encounters with actual Blackfullas. You'll find these executively Indigenous types are more likely to use their powers to investigate claims of lateral violence among the Blacks than they are the acts of racism among the whites, and they will replace vacated positions with more and more of the ambiguous Aborigines who are unlikely to question the cultural credentials they flaunt.

They hold healing circles and they like to 'yarn' with message sticks instead of talk in staff meetings, adorning the place with Indigenous art and artefacts, while ensuring there are fewer Indigenous people to disrupt the standard order of things. Beware the Indigenising moment of singular and senior appointments in white institutions; it is an illusion of progress working to disguise the ongoing colonial violence Blackfullas are being subject to ... and tragically it's working.

humiliated them instead

Once upon a time our ancestors were deemed the last of their tribe. Today they call us the firsts of our tribe. Whether first or last, the agenda is identical. The colonisers have long relied upon the myth of us as a doomed race destined to die out. That disingenuous lament of 'the last of their tribe', having massacred our people, represents a form of elimination in what Patrick Wolfe refers to as an 'organizing principle of settler–colonial society'.[8] Yet generation after generation, our ancestors, those supposed 'last of their tribe' types, still manage to keep reproducing more of their tribe. Much like the coloniser sciences that seek to know when we 'arrived' here but find with every new research investment they 'discover' that we were here far longer than they first imagined. Indigenous presence has really messed with the coloniser account of things. Their preoccupation with the Black body, in its absence and presence as first or last, is not about our ancestry, our capabilities, or just a matter of archaeological inquiry; it is about our land and contesting our rightful claim to it.

The first-generation Aborigine types are literally the firsts of their tribe but they too herald the end of the tribe – in that they are not connected to an actual tribe, and any affiliation as Indigenous is via a disadvantage that can be remedied, most typically by a white patron or white institution. The colonisers have not relinquished their attachment to the idea that we are destined to die out, with the remnants of the tribe to be absorbed into the coloniser population. That is why it is often the coloniser who is most excited by the discovery of the firsts of their tribes. In a 'settler move to innocence',[9] they can lay claim to saving us while solving the Aboriginal problem through a statistical absorption into the mainstream.

In any colonial institution, we can witness the ritualistic stocktake of Black bodies, whether in annual reports, KPIs, or those reconciliation action plan committee meetings. The talk is of numbers: numbers recruited and numbers retained. Having worked only in Indigenous spaces I have sat in so many of those meetings, where Indigenous sovereignty is supplanted with a grotesque kind of Black body count. This is the problem of supposed Indigenising agendas grounded in equity rather than sovereignty.

I remember working with a faculty in an academic institution that had no Indigenous staff but was among the faculties with the highest numbers of Indigenous students. When questioned on this discrepancy, one staff member explained that there was a senior faculty member who was Indigenous but she chose not to identify. I still remember the look of shock on the staff member's face when I said, 'Well, you can't count her.'

You see the story of addressing supposed Indigenous disadvantage (as opposed to recognising Indigenous sovereignty) is a story of benevolence and progress concocted by the colonisers, and to make that story true, they need not change their systems or structures, but simply change how they count who is Indigenous. And this is the problem with the influx of the ambiguously Indigenous; they are being enlisted to maintain the status quo. Whether an institution speaks of reconciliation, decolonisation or Indigenisation, it all comes down to a matter of maths, where the end goal is parity in lieu of Indigenous sovereignty, via an Indigenousness from nowhere in particular.

Through the 'first of their tribe' they can now joyfully speak of the vanishing Aborigines and, unlike those lasts, they are all too happy to claim credit for having produced them; most typically through the mentorship and capacity- and aspiration-building programs our young people are being indoctrinated into. It is the newly identifying Aborigine who is most susceptible to these programs because it is often the first 'Indigenous space' in which they get to do their identity work. Yet it is an Indigenous space that has been constructed by colonisers. You will find that the ontologically Indigenous don't last long in those programs. They get kicked out or moved on for being too outspoken; that is, too Black.

The firsts of their tribe are enlisted as the public relations arm of the colonial project, not just that major bank, mining company, government department or academic institution.

They are the shiny fresh faces of mainstreaming/dispersal agendas, literally and figuratively. The phenotypical Aborigine or even ethnically ambiguous Aborigine who is ontologically white is the most prized of all as they embody the Indigenousness that colonisers want. These happy faces feature on any and all Indigenising promotional agendas where 'the natives' are encouraged to aspire to be just like them, who too aspired to be just like the good white folk, and who eventually 'made it'. You will note that 'making it' typically means completing a course, a task or a traineeship, rather than effecting change in the conditions of Blackfullas beyond their own. But through this, the colonisers look all the more virtuous in their violence.

The firsts of their tribe types always have a white patron who got them there, and she is typically a white woman. The virtuous white woman has always had her sights on our children and it is the ambiguously Indigenous who they set their sights on, because they are more capable of being cultivated in their image. I've seen white women do all kinds of things to ensure the ambiguously Indigenous person is counted as Indigenous while knowing full well that their claims are incomplete and/ or unsubstantiated. But rescuing or rather claiming Black children is a well-worn path for white women and has long been part of the civilising colonial project.

It's why so many Indigenous youth mentoring programs are so deeply problematic. They are always conceived of on their terms, a criterion of their deciding what it is to be an Indigenous leader and what constitutes leadership. Most of these programs are the training grounds for the next intake of native police and it's why white corporations, rather than Black communities, are resourced to provide them.

Once upon a time the vanishing Aborigine could be explained away via those exemption certificates, alongside the litany of infectious diseases on death certificates. Today we have confirmation of Aboriginality certificates or, worse, statutory declarations of self-identification. The need to count more people as Indigenous is not in the interests of actual advancement but enables the illusion of advancement.

The story of statistical advancement, which often stresses the first of the tribe over the rest of the tribe, accessorises colonial institutions just like those flags do. They supposedly signal the institution's inclusiveness, a sign of progress, which operates more like 'nothing more to see here' in terms of the colonial violence perpetuated by said institutions. The numbers supposedly tell this story, yet we know that all that has changed is how they define those who get counted as Indigenous. What is more inclusive is not the institution, but the definition of Indigeneity – which certainly has expanded markedly from the blood-quantum kind into which my father was born.

The mythical Aborigine from elsewhere or nowhere serves the myth-making about progress and benevolence of the colony of this generation's time. And we have a generation of Blackfullas, who have grown up under the premise and promise of closing the gap, mainstreaming agendas of the state, not knowing any other way of being. Too many have bought into the idea that an Indigeneity articulated under the rubric of diversity and disadvantage is emancipatory, because they are escapable conditions achieved through the aid of white women. But there is no escaping Indigenous sovereignty; well, only if you have forgotten who you are and where you come from.

as we grew up we felt alone

I remember my father always saying, 'No matter what, never forget who you are and where you come from.' As a child I used to think of it as one of his sayings, but it was more than that – it was a fundamental truth that would ground me in place, at the highest of my highs and the lowest of my lows. It helped me remember the truth of things in a place that has only ever lied about us and them. It protects us against the violence of those colonial-settler myths upon our bodies and souls – that we aren't from here, that we weren't here, and that we won't be here for much longer. This is why we need our people to remember. This is not a matter of the first of the tribe versus the rest of the tribe, but a matter of survival of the tribe in a colonial-settler state. If you do not know, then you need to find out who you are and where you come from – as an act of resistance and survival at least, to ensure that you are not cast in that most hopeless role of all: the last of your tribe.

The sad truth is that there are those who are legitimately or illegitimately claiming a connection that is less about a belonging to Indigenous peoples or lands and more to do with procuring a sense of belonging within white institutions. Some are too comfortable occupying the role of both first and last of their tribe, because it means there is no-one to be held accountable to, or to be in relationship to, so one can make it up on the run, because they are all too comfortable with being 'the one'. For these people Aboriginality is claimed as a thing to be discovered and possessed, as opposed to a way of being in the world. These are the people who seek out and trade upon the confirmation of Aboriginality as an actual confirmation of their identity, as though the document has some kind of currency outside of engagement with the state and its resources.

It is why we are wary of people who discover their identity and immediately seek out a confirmation of Aboriginality before seeking out a relationship with those Black relatives and Black lands. A confirmation of Aboriginality document is a way of dealing with the state to verify entitlement to something reserved for Aboriginal people. People can be Aboriginal without it and many are – always have been, always will be. Thus it is okay to seek belonging and connection, to return to your people and your community without claiming anything but a sense of belonging. In fact it is absolutely necessary to identify yourself to your mob. But this should be before declaring it to the white institution you are seeking validation from.

That sense of belonging that Indigenous communities offer is really something, no matter where that Indigenous community exists. I have been welcomed into many Aboriginal communities to which I don't have bloodline connection and it is a privilege that I would never take for granted. Nor would I overstep the mark about what it means. You see, belonging, while a gift, is not an entitlement one can claim or use to claim.

We are a relational people and as such visitors will be accounted for and situated within the social order – and I am not just talking of skin names and the remote Aboriginal community context. It's why I don't trust people who say they attempted to rebuild relationships with their own mob but were turned away.

You see my mother is white and in being family she is afforded all sorts of privileges in her proximity to Indigenous peoples; she is called Aunty and she is included in all manner of community cultural life, but that is not a one-way street. She also is called upon to help with this and that, man the stall, help fix someone's bridesmaid dress. 'Just call Aunty Elaine,' they say. And even for all of that she remains white, and when encountering people in community contexts she is sure to remind them that she is white so there's no mistaking. But that's not always the case. I've heard white mothers of Black children speak on Indigenous issues more broadly – and invoking the pronoun of 'we'.

There are white people who via proximity get a taste of belonging in an Indigenous sense and, such is their identity crisis as colonisers on stolen land, they seek desperately to belong. Simply being in relationship to Indigenous peoples is not enough to satisfy their appetite. Proximity to is not the same as *being* and these types know that to be true. To speak of belonging to this place Indigenously is something that cannot be claimed in the same way.[10]

The oft-cited 'it's not who you claim but who claims you' rejects the idea that Indigenousness is a feeling that one has. To be Indigenous is in the being, the social location among

Indigenous peoples which is determined via bloodlines to country. But there remains non-Indigenous and ambiguously Indigenous peoples who are claimed by Indigenous families. In these cases we see those individuals using family location to claim a universal Indigeneity beyond the family social setting.

Further, we also witness 'bubs' who have been found and re-located within their cultural context but who use the newfound position to place themselves in broader Indigenous leadership roles in ways their communities are oblivious to and don't necessarily endorse. It requires us to think more deeply not just about who is claiming who, but who is claiming what and how and when and where.

and one sweet day all the children came back

It is often difficult to speak publicly about people who are discovering their Aboriginality and not just because of the dangers of identity talk in the public domain because of how it gets used by right-wing commentators. When we speak of the violence of the children who have come back, we are accused of not being respectful of the trauma suffered by the stolen generations, as though there are some Blackfullas out here who have managed to be unaffected by colonial violence.

It is important to note that when we speak of the newly identifying Aborigine, we typically are not speaking of the stolen generations and their descendants whose story has been stolen, but those who for generations have been disconnected. Yet there is an instructiveness in the anthem of the stolen generation, Archie Roach's 'Took the Children Away'.[11] He speaks so clearly to the racial indoctrination of the stolen generation in being taught all the white man's ways and being taught prejudice. What isn't spoken about is how this internalised racial violence is inflicted upon our families and communities by those who have been 'acting white, yet feeling Black'. He certainly sings of the sweet day when 'all the children come back'. But he sings of a return 'back where their hearts grow strong, back where they all belong', which is not to the white institution. The children, he sings, return back to their mothers, fathers, sisters, brothers, people and land. It is only through connecting back to Black family, community and country that one's heart can grow strong.

Archie sings too of 'children' returning. And in their returning as children they have much to learn before claiming titles of elders or leaders. It is those who refuse to come to learn from the Aboriginal and Torres Strait Islander families and communities that they've been estranged from who are called out, and rightly so. Sadly these children in centring themselves end up throwing tantrums the moment they are called to be accountable as a member of the tribe rather than a self-appointed leader. In doing so, they've missed the fact that there is something special about being a member of the tribe, more special than being the first, and certainly more special than any piece of paper. There is no shame in being one of the mob because it is such an important place to be. This is what it is to be via being in relation with others, rather than a concocted colonial account of us.

chelsea watego

It is those who don't have a connection to mob who have difficulty dealing with Black accountability. They construct Black critique as violent, which is yet another example of the racist imaginings that shape their world, one in which Black people don't deserve shit, let alone the right to demand better than what's on offer. Here, Indigenous ancestry is deployed not as a way of being in the world, but as a defence against being held accountable culturally, intellectually and politically to Blackfullas. It is these mob who are often most indignant about being of service to, or answerable to, the members of the community to which they've just claimed entry. Their supposed Indigenous ancestry privileges them in terms of what can be said to white folk about what it is to be Aboriginal, and their whiteness means they have proximity to power in ways that the sovereign Aboriginal will never seek. They've simply known no other way, having not been raised in Aboriginal homes or communities. So the idea of learning from and/or answering to the people they had been too shame to associate with often can be too hard for them to comprehend. Having never been taught, they cannot see the limitation of their knowing and will refuse to because they've always accepted the idea that Aboriginal people occupy the most inferior status and couldn't possibly teach them anything.

I still remember sister Teila Watson speaking of those who don't know the humility of relationality and she described it in terms of those who've never had to serve cups of tea to their Elders. I still laugh at the time I was humiliated by my nanna for serving her weak tea at my father's wake. And, look, in my defence I don't drink tea or coffee, but when Nanna asks for a cup of tea, you better well learn how to make it. But in that moment I was to discover the limitations of my knowing, when Nanna declared loudly, 'I've seen dirty dishwater darker than that.' Thankfully my older sister stepped in to save the day but, as Teila points out, it is in those moments that we are reminded who we are here for, who we are meant to be of service to. This event was also a stark reminder that our Elders never settled for weak tea.

back where they all belong

I am not suggesting that those who don't know who they are or where they come from don't have a place in our communities, so please spare me the angry and tearful email, phone call, group chat, or lawsuit. All that is being asked is that you find and know your place before claiming to know on behalf of the rest of us. And it is from Blackfullas that you will learn that, not via the Indigenous appointments of white institutions. And, yes, being in relationship with mob is an ongoing everyday kind of thing – it is a way of being in the world.

From my observations, Blackfullas have always been welcoming of the stolen children returning. The scepticism surrounds those who claim a home that they never actually return to, or move to, but expect to be treated like a special guest. What is being asked of you is to do the work that everyone else has to do. Being Black after all is a way of being – it is not an entitlement and most definitely isn't a free pass. You have work to do, just like the rest of us, and it's not okay to be indignant at having to be of service to Black people, unless of course you think that's a lesser kind of service.

Your presence and your working through how to be a member of the tribe should not be traumatising to the Blackfullas who have been holding things down on the home front while you were living among the whitefullas. There's a place for you and you will find it, but only through investing in building relationships with your own mob, whichever ones of them that you can find. And when you do, you will own your story in such a way that you will know from what place you speak, and the limitations of it, and you will declare it, so no-one else will have to call you out – again, just like the rest of us.

Also, it is okay to be a guest if you want to be. You can reference ancestry while acknowledging that you don't share that lived social identity. It's just like behaving as one would in another's house and not making out you own it. I have Irish heritage and I've never claimed myself to be Irish or professed to know what that is. If you don't feel strong in your own identity story of being Aboriginal, that's okay, but the work you do is up to you. Other Blackfullas should never be used as your punching bag.

We too are still theorising what it means to be Indigenous in this place, for our own children and communities amid the ongoing dispossession we are subject to. Sadly so much of our labour is exhausted in undoing the damage caused by those who claim authority to know in ways that undermine our ways of knowing, being, doing and living as a people.

For those among you who are working out the difference between *having* Indigenous ancestry and *being* Indigenous, or have yet to realise there is a difference, there is work to be done. There is a difference between an Indigenousness that is expressed as a past possession and that which is a way of being in the world. You don't get to extract other people's stories, histories, languages or mannerisms to pass off an Indigeneity that doesn't belong to you. It is embodied, and that means working out who you are in being Indigenous to the people and land you claim so that you may know then how to be in relationship with other mob, including those you've just reconnected with. Finding out where you sit is your responsibility and not the responsibility of others.

The relationship that must be attended to, as Langton pointed out, 'is not between actual Aboriginal people'[12] but instead with the symbols created by the colonisers, the very people you once thought yourself to be. Questions of identity thus run far deeper than skin colour. And that identity crisis is not born out of a lack of love and acceptance from Blackfullas. It is the product of a proximity to whiteness. Tragically there are some who refuse to give up that relationship, whose being in the world is still predicated upon the love and acceptance from white people, white institutions and white power. It is those people who will forever remain individually, ambitiously, occupationally and ambiguously Indigenous.

6

fuck hope

TRANSCRIPT OF PROCEEDINGS

MAGISTRATES COURT

KELLY, Magistrate

MAG-0034368/19(8) and MAG-00132185/19(1)

POLICE	Complainant
and	
CHELSEA JOANNE RUTH BOND	Defendant

BRISBANE

10.16 AM, MONDAY, 15 JULY 2019

DAY 1

DECISION

BENCH: Ms Bond, you have pleaded guilty at an early stage to a charge of commit-public-nuisance, and I note that other two existing charges before the Court were not proceeded with by the Prosecution today. I take into account that very early
5 plea. I've heard limited facts with respect to it, but ultimately – on the night of the 1st of December, you created public nuisance by arguing loudly with a gentleman outside a nightclub after you'd been – after that premises had been shut. You are an educated lady. You're mother of five children, who are aged from 16 and below. You're heavily involved in your community, and you travel for your work. You've
10 also been involved in the foundation of an organisation. What I take from the facts is that the argument caused sufficient concern to people within the vicinity that they made their way around you and the gentleman arguing.

Taking into account the facts of the matter and your personal circumstances – there is
15 a conviction back in 2000, which is now nearly 19 years ago. So that is irrelevant for my purposes today. I've listened to Mr Hoare's submissions. I do, taking into account the facts in the matter and your personal circumstances, consider it appropriate, that no punishment or only a nominal punishment should be imposed. It's therefore ordered, that you be released absolutely, and no conviction is recorded.
20 I hope very much, though, Ms Bond, that you don't find yourself back before the Court with respect to this type of offence or any other type of offence and that the incident would not be repeated by you.

Unmitigated Blackness is coming to the realization that as fucked up and meaningless as it all is, sometimes it's the nihilism that makes life worth living.

Paul Beatty[1]

Edward Said in *Representations of the Intellectual* reminds us that 'there is a special duty to address the constituted and authorised powers of one's own society, which is accountable to its citizenry, particularly when those powers are exercised in a manifestly disproportionate and immoral war, or in a deliberate program of discrimination, repression and collective cruelty.'[2] As an Aboriginal academic it is necessary that my language be clear.

fuck hope

I've always been curious about hope and the insistence that Blackfullas have it, of all things – often as the only thing. As a child, hope seemed to be something reserved for white people, those families on Ramsay Street or other such pleasant cul-de-sacs who had matching lounge-room chairs and coffee tables, who got dropped to school in cars with air conditioning, comforted in knowing it would never break down on the way to anywhere. Hope to me has always worked for the folks for whom everything turns up trumps, through whatever adversity they meet. Hope was never for the hopeless. It was always the stuff of fairy tales and fables, which were reserved exclusively for white people and, occasionally, those respectable ethnics.

I remember complaining to my white mother repeatedly as a child about things not being fair, to which she would reply so matter-of-factly, 'Life isn't fair.' I hated that answer because it wasn't fair to me that life wasn't fair, and especially because I knew it was for some. I saw the differential treatment in the everyday encounters of my white mother and Black father in the social world we occupied.

But it is not as though I wanted the things that white people possessed; I remember wanting to break through that 'vast veil' in the way Du Bois³ refused to. I did not want their stuff – I wanted their sight. I wanted to be able to see the world as they saw it, that real gift of sight; which actually isn't that second sight of seeing yourself through the eyes of a world that 'views you with contempt and pity'. No, I wanted that gift of sight they had: the fundamental belief in the goodness of the social world one occupies, of thinking that the world and all within it was within your reach, and the confidence of knowing that the world will work for you, because of course it is founded upon your humanity too. But for Blackfullas it isn't. Never was and never will be, at least in the colony.

We occupy a social world that refuses to see our humanity, and not because it has yet to discover it, but precisely because its very existence is founded upon our violent erasure. It has no other way of knowing itself. When I speak of erasure I speak of it in a literal sense beyond that of the absence of representation or inclusion or of a past violence. On any given day, in any given place, you can be guaranteed that most if not all colonisers would have no idea whose land they are walking, working or talking on, such is their way of being in the world. And, the thing is, they really need not know for them to exist in this place. Our erasure is rendered irrelevant to them, precisely because of its relevance to them.

When we acknowledge country as Blackfullas, in particular country that is not ours, we are invoking a protocol that has been fundamental to our coexistence for well over 60,000 years. This act foregrounds Indigenous presence everywhere all the time, not just ourselves but that of other nations. But this is a difference between a colonising people and a relational people. Among the colonisers we see an appetite for a type of Aboriginal culture that can be possessed, a consumable culture of arts and artefacts, rather than an embracing of cultural practices that foregrounds Indigenous presence as ongoing and unceded.

They will never realise our humanity, no matter how many reconciliation action plans, race discrimination cases or special research funding rounds they establish. And there is a real danger in entertaining any of the 'performative illusions'[4] of Indigenous inclusion or appreciation, either aspirational or actual, in the colony. So I want instead to make a case for nihilism, as defined by Paul Beatty's character FK Me in the book *The Sellout*.[5]

The lead character, the son of FK Me, is raised in a ghetto on the outskirts of Los Angeles by his single father, who exposes him to 'racially charged psychological studies' which supposedly would 'lead to a memoir to solve the family's financial woes'. However, there is no memoir, and when his father is killed in a police shooting all he is left with is the trauma of being a Black subject, and his father's funeral bill.

The novel is lauded as a 'searing satire'[6] but for Black subjects who are crowdfunding family funerals on a daily basis, there is nothing satirical about *The Sellout*. Indeed, Beatty himself insists that the book is neither comedy nor satire, but it does go to show, when Black people tell stories of their social world, it can never be believed in the same way white fictions of Black lives are.

Angela Davis reminds us of the importance of Black literature when she insists that it provides a 'much more illuminating account ... than all the philosophical discourses' on theorising about freedom precisely because 'it projects the consciousness of a people who have been denied entrance into the real world of freedom'.[7]

Before he dies, FK Me's father, a Black social scientist, theorised different types or stages of Black consciousness. This framework for thinking through Blackness isn't all that fictional and was shaped by Beatty's undergraduate studies in psychology where he encountered the work of Black psychologist William E Cross. These stages of Blackness, as reimagined by Beatty through the character of FK Me, are outlined thus:

The stage I of Blackness is the 'Neophyte Negro' who,

according to Beatty, 'is afraid of his own blackness. A blackness that feels incapable, infinite and less than … He or she wants to be anything but black.'[8] They want to be white because they've come to believe 'white is right'. This is what I would refer to as the Sam Thaiday 'jungle fever joke'[9] type of Blackness. It loathes and ridicules the Black body, the same Black body it insists can only exist when it is validated by the white people, institutions and power that surround it.

The stage II form of Blackness is the 'Capital B Black'. According to Beatty, the distinguishing feature is 'a heightened awareness of race. Here race is still all-consuming, but in a more positive fashion.'[10] This is the black is beautiful form of Blackness. It is the Black and deadly form of Blackness that is a claim and a contestation that doesn't necessarily change our location. This is the commercialised capitalist B kind of Blackness which operates aesthetically as 'I'm Aboriginal but I'm not *insert every negative stereotype about Aboriginal people*'. In all of its positivity it cannot see how anti-Black it is, in how it negates and demonises actual Black people who cannot adhere to this reimagined superhuman, supermodel form of Blackness.

The stage III type of Blackness is that of 'Race Transcendentalism'. Beatty's character describes it as, 'A collective consciousness that fights oppression and seeks serenity … Examples of stage III black folks are people like Rosa Parks, Harriet Tubman, Sitting Bull … They are the woman on your left, the man on your right. It's overcoming racial oppression and making everything right, as if there is such a place where everything will be right.'[11] It is so positively superiorly Black that it refuses to recognise any critiques as anything but jealousy and toxicity.

Rather than a destination, we find ourselves on a constant journey, the constant struggle for serenity, a serenity which many of us have imagined is found at mountain tops. The mountain-top Blacks are those deemed the 'next Martin Luther King' types who are heralded as visionaries for transcending racism. This is the courtroom battles kind of Blackness, 'the '67 Referendum was a sign of progress' kind of Blackness. Mountain-top Blacks experience racism or anti-racism as a moment of singular causes or cases, in a place where they've come to believe race is aberrational rather than foundational. Consequently, one's existence is bound up in the belief that one sweet day, in one sweet move, race will be overcome. Yet, ironically, the arrival of such a day still rests entirely upon having hope in white patrons and white adjudicators for emancipation.

But who could blame us for seeking those Martin Luther King mountain-top moments having been fed a diet of civil rights movies from the US where we can count on justice to arrive just before the credits roll. It is an alluring narrative; so much so, it is a place that many of us have lived in and tragically died prematurely by believing in, or forever been tormented by having finally realised the futility of being in.

But Beatty's character insists that there should be a stage IV of Black identity, which he describes as 'Unmitigated Blackness'. He says, 'I'm not sure what Unmitigated Blackness is, but whatever it is, it doesn't sell. On the surface Unmitigated Blackness is a seeming unwillingness to succeed. It's the serious black actor.

It's a night in jail. Unmitigated Blackness is simply not giving a fuck.'[12] It's the Tarneen Onus-Williams 'burn it down' kind of Blackness. Unmitigated Blackness, Beatty states, 'is coming to the realization that as fucked up and meaningless as it all is, sometimes it's the nihilism that makes life worth living.'

Nihilism that makes life worth living is a proposition I have thought about for some time intellectually and ontologically.[13] It was at my darkest moments that I found solace in it, as well as courage. While there is something freeing about no longer giving a fuck, I don't think I necessarily found the freedom in it that was promised, because the strength of not giving a fuck typically feels most possible once there's nothing left to lose. Yet unmitigated Blackness is the closest thing to an embodied sovereignty that I have heard articulated.

There really is an underestimation of the violence of living in a world that wishes you dead, which, in your living, refuses to see you and, even in your excellence, renders you invisible or undeserving. There isn't an escape from that place, even if for a few moments here and there they grant you entry to their world. And after a while you can't help but question the point of it all, in all of its meaningless. Yet in speaking of Unmitigated Blackness there appeared to be a possibility in the nihilism that Beatty's character offered – a reason for living, for working and for fighting. Having spoken to Blackfullas across the country about nihilism, I saw a power in the possibility of it that was not present in all the talk of hope.

It is the everydayness of race in being part of the air that we breathe[14] that means it is routinely suffocating, particularly for those racialised as Black *and* Indigenous in a colonial-settler society. This is the reason that all of us Blackfullas find it hard to breathe some days, to the point that to be in a constant struggle of gasping for air can be too overwhelming a burden to bear.

I remember a dear friend describing how, in his darkest days, he longed for the free-ness of the air rushing past his face as he jumped off the Story Bridge to his death. There is no mystery as to why suicide and self-harm are among the leading causes of death of our people. There is a present and ongoing impossibility of *being* Black in this place that they created. It is they who deemed us incapable of existing, of living, and of being authentically Indigenous in this place, in this time. Some might attribute suicide rates in our communities to the result of having given up hope, the endgame of being bereft of it. I would argue it's a result of our reliance upon it.

fuck hope

To survive, some of our mob have thought they needed to cling to hope. The Race Transcendentalist relies on the hope of winning, or of incremental progress, while trying to outrun race. The Capital B Blacks hope that eventually, one day, the colonisers will come to see their humanity too, if they are just pretty enough, cool enough, mainstream enough. They hope that their cultural awareness workshop or the latest documentary or book will turn those white supremacists around. Those who take up the position of race blindness are also relying on the hope that, despite all evidence to the contrary, race isn't real. They hope that if they play down their Blackness enough, others will entertain the delusion so that they may be permitted to take a seat at the table. There doesn't appear to be any possibility of a Black hope independent of white patronage, of white fans, white followers, white likes and white lies.

Hope is a most ridiculous strategy for Blackfullas in the colony precisely because it doesn't actually do anything – for us. It relies upon a false sense of respite from the reality of everyday racial violence in the colony; that we suspend all logic and cling to hope, a waiting for a future good while living in a permanent hell. It tells us to wait, that one day we will get our turn. It tells us that we aren't worth fighting for right now, but what it doesn't tell us is that day never actually arrives. Hope is a suspension of Black trauma in the midst of Black trauma, and a premature death sentence for those destined to be betrayed by it.

Whenever I have spoken to colonisers about the retiring of hope, I have been met with indignation, outrage and patronising concern. Some people may think that calls to retire hope for nihilism are irresponsible. But what is irresponsible is to require us to maintain the status quo of keeping Black bodies connected to life support machines they've been deemed never capable of getting off. Hope is a poor excuse for a pacifier: barely soothing, let alone offering any sustenance for survival. It is the new smoothing of the pillow of the dying, a call to wait for a new day which never dawns. Every year in parliament we are called to witness their statistical account of our demise as ongoing, as inevitable and as inescapable.

But this is the function of hope in a colonial-settler state. Like role models, capacity-building agendas, reconciliation action plans and an Indigenousness derived from nowhere, hope offers up change without change. This is why colonisers are so insistent we have it – hope is not an enabler of our existence, but of theirs. It is not a vehicle of Black emancipation – it is a psychological tool of the coloniser to insist that we accept things the way they are, forevermore. It is a means by which we come to accept our supposed inferior status and deem ourselves not worthy of better, where we accept an existence predicated upon waiting passively for our humanity to be seen. But that waiting place is useless.

For almost every condition for which there is data, we are more likely to get it, get sicker from it and die earlier because of it. Hope has not helped us. It is killing us because for too long we've invested in the idea of waiting for it. I'm no longer waiting on, or celebrating, incremental forms of progress, so-called well-intentioned steps in the right direction, which always seem to fail us. This failure, we are told, should be met with more hope, as though it is our fault for not having enough of it, as though one can wish oneself out of oppressive social structures. The truth is, hope sedates the logical response of anger and outrage that fuels Black insistence.

fuck hope

Those colonisers most horrified by the prospect of retiring hope have never sat at the kitchen tables of Blackfullas where guest lists for funerals have been drafted well before someone meets their death, where a return to the creator is yearned for, where tears have been cried into cups of tea for a justice that will never be achieved, not only in one's lifetime, but ever. Retiring hope is not a giving up, but a matter of a turning up each day in truth.

Jimmy Chi, when he sang 'There's nothing I would rather be', cuts through the bullshit of positivity and hopefulness of being Black. A song that appears on the surface one of pride about being Aboriginal – in the 'Black is beautiful' kind of way, with its upbeat tempo and happy faces – actually tells a fairly ugly truth about our existence in this place.

> There's nothing I would rather be than to be an Aborigine
> And dream of just what heaven must be like.
> And finally when I die I know I'll be going up, cos you know
>   that I've had my hell on earth.

Ever since I can remember I knew about death and dying. Actually, worse than that, I was reminded quite regularly about the impending end of the earth, also known as the end times. The end times were always so imminent, but ironically it was not in a doom-and-gloom kind of way – the end times brought as much promise as the 'bran nue dae' that Jimmy Chi sang about.

You see, it was during the visits from my evangelical Aboriginal grandmother when she would journey up to Brisbane from Tweed Heads, or vice versa, that we would sit around the table and even the most mundane observation about the weather would be cause for Nanna to lament over her tea about the end times, only to follow up with this cheerful smile across her face about the glory of the Lord and flying horses or something or other. It conjured up a kind of never-ending story, figuratively and literally. The end times meant salvation for those who had suffered, and retribution for those remorseless sinners. Death was never seen as the end. Death was a transition to somewhere else, and there seemed to be a certainty that it would be somewhere better, that our suffering on earth was a kind of surety that we were destined for better things.

My colleague Bryan Mukandi and I have previously ruminated on Uncle Roger Knox's 'Warrior in Chains', a song of a Black man in a prison cell who could no longer cope with being incarcerated.[15] Knox, in song, tells the story of the Black prisoner beside his cell who, in life, is unable to sing his song of freedom. The song speaks of the tragedy of suicide, and the reality that the song of freedom could only ring loudly in the prisoner's death.

It brings to mind Briggs's video of 'Life Is Incredible', which features young Aboriginal people dropping dead around him and in the final moments we are led to believe he is next, with the only person surviving being the elderly white man. It is such a powerful representation of the reality for Blackfullas in the colony every day. The aged care facility representing the paternalistic palliative care approach so prevalent in Indigenous affairs where white people preside daily over premature deaths so matter-of-factly, just as they do in annual closing the gap reporting.

That report each year isn't just a story of policy failure; it is a coloniser commemoration, disguised as commiseration, of their system working as it should, hence the 'refresh' of a decade-long failed strategy. This framework of data collection dressed up as a strategy functions to produce a fiction of racial inferiority, rather than tell the truth of the mechanisms that produce racial inequality.[16] There is no escape from the violence of colonialism, not even in the things meant to serve our interests.

Kobie Dee, like my nanna, Knox and Chi, also sings of the peace found in death for Blackfullas. His song for cousin Jody, who is shot during an armed hold-up by a security guard, sounds much like the sorrow songs of slaves that Du Bois speaks of. Such songs, he states, 'grope toward some unseen power and sigh for rest in the End'.[17]

Kobie sings of his cousin Jody in the moment of his death:

He just looks up to the sky and smiles in pride,
He's happy he can finally die,
Cause he could never do it himself,
He never thought that a soul would even dare to help,
And so we pray that he rests in peace
Cause we're just happy that he finally made it out of the streets.[18]

For a people who are dying disproportionately, daily, prematurely, unjustly and horrifically, it's little wonder we

201

might have something to say about it. But this talk of death and end is not a summons for it to come sooner. It is a form of truth-telling about the social world we occupy in all of its hopelessness. Du Bois in his analysis of sorrow songs argues it's the music of an 'unhappy people, of the children of disappointment which tell of death and suffering and unvoiced longing toward a truer world'.[19]

There is this yearning for a truer world, perhaps because, as Chi points out, the truth of this place is too ugly. In making the case for the musical *Bran Nue Dae*, Chi suggested that the truth should instead be dressed up in the finery of parable. I am unconvinced that we are best served by this dressing-up of truth because I think, even in its ugliness, it is still the most generous expression of love. Hope, for me, has come to represent a dressing-up of Black truth that masks our reality and makes us numb to the brutality of it all. Hope thus functions to enable white lies, rather than to better Black lives. To speak the truth to Black people about Black people is an act of love for Black people, even when that truth is ugly, and perhaps especially when it is.

Those lies we live with, that we think our existence is dependent upon, visit much harm upon our people. After all, race itself is a lie that we've been forced to live with, and the violence of it has included the entertainment of it in our minds, as though it tells a truth about our capabilities as a people. It tells us that if we only behaved or performed better we could escape the brutality of it, that if we worked harder they would include us, that if we ate more vegetables and exercised more we would outlive it, that if we just accepted things and moved on, it would disappear. But it's not true.

I've seen the heartbreak of Blackfullas who at one level know the violence visited upon them by the institution, but who still replay their supposed missteps of resistance and protection. I know too many fierce Blackfullas immobilised by this thinking. The myth of racial uplift has been yet another lie and form of racial violence visited upon Black people, not helped by those who sustain it, both Black and white.

The first Black American president famously wrote about hope and the supposed audacity of it, as though it were something courageous. He defined hope as not a matter of blind optimism but as 'a belief in things not seen … [and] a belief that there are better days ahead'. But the truth is, there are no better days ahead, nor are there bran nue daes; there are just more days, all of which are the sum total of another day in the colony. Why must we speak of the stuff of fairy tales when we are trapped in a dystopian world, anyway?

Once upon a time, my favourite poems of Aboriginal activist and poet Oodgeroo Noonuccal were 'Song of Hope' and 'Son of Mine'. Those poems articulated a refusal to sing of hatred and heartbreak, and instead spoke of hope and new horizons.[20] She wasn't singing of fairy tales, I'm most certain, for this was the 1970s, a time of rapid social change locally and globally of which Blackfullas were finally beneficiaries too. I can appreciate her optimism as the world underwent some fairly rapid social changes: Blackfullas emerging from the protectionist policies that had incarcerated and enslaved us across the state to move into towns, even if at the fringes; Black children getting entry to white schools and pools; laws created that made race discrimination illegal. It is no wonder Blackfullas at that time sang of hope. As a child born on the eve of the 1980s, I knew the ideology of hopes, dreams, and new days and dawns all too well.

I come from that place of possibility of racial uplift, of working ten times harder to obtain inclusion and breaking through the veil not to sing of hope, but to speak of the exhaustion and disappointment of it all. I come from the place of innumerable firsts (finishing high school, graduating university, home ownership), but I know it has only been in a Steven Bradbury kind of way. That is, it is not because I am any better than those who have come before me, or that white people have become more generous; it is just the conditions which denied those before me have been removed, and primarily through Black insistence rather than through having held out hope in white institutions.

Further, these so-called achievements of entering into white institutions for the first time are an inclusion that works as an illusion of race transcendentalism. Those firsts are not signs of progress but are 'settler moves to innocence'.[21] We are granted entry into their institutions only when said entry is considered unlikely to destabilise the narrative of the world they have constructed for themselves, while making them appear inclusive and welcoming. Yet, we all know, should other Blacks ever question the work of the sole Black in those places when it's time to take a side between Blackfullas and colonisers, we will be swiftly shut down and told to mark as emancipatory this most assimilatory form of 'progress'. It is why the presence of Lidia Thorpe in federal parliament, regardless of how contradictory some may claim her position to be, is a most refreshing spectacle for Blackfullas to see, given the unmitigated nature of her Blackness in the chamber.

The more recent aspirations of the colony to include us in health, education and employment opportunities is not for our benefit but theirs. The policy story they tell, which has been around for over a decade now, of Black 'children to school and parents to work and safer communities', is a way of appearing to solve the Aboriginal problem while upholding white virtue and white power. We still haven't got our land back and they still don't deem us worthy of the category of human. We remain an equity project capable of being remedied once we make it to the middle class, but even that hasn't changed shit.

The truth is, anything that has been won here has been long fought for by Blackfullas and anything that has been achieved has been watered down by whitefullas. Race, and the violence of it, remains as ever before. It has just had to articulate itself differently, to appear less apparent. This is why celebrating racial progress is absurd to me. No matter how high we climb, how hard we work, there is no point in holding out hope in them – entry into their world comes at a price, and even when we have paid in full, they still withdraw it at any time they please. Typically those most protected by hope in white institutions will insist that those of us who aren't just didn't have what it takes. Yet it is in having returned from that place, of moving from the fringes to the firsts, of making it to mountain tops, that I refuse to sing of hope, and instead call upon its retirement as a strategy for Black emancipation.

fuck hope

Retiring hope is a strategy, not simply of a Black insistence on truth-telling but a strategy for living. In retiring hope for nihilism I'm not suggesting that death is our only way out, nor am I suggesting that we are living an ontological death. I am thinking here not of Black life as social death; rather I'm interested in a Black life that is lived. And I am most certain that there is a Black existence and a Black future available to us, beyond the present binary of white lies and Black deaths.

To retire hope is not a matter of pessimism, Afro or otherwise – it is a trading in truth-telling that is foundational to our survival. Beatty says it's the nihilism that makes life worth living. Nihilism here is about a way of living – and it is via truth that living is made possible. A truth not only of the futility of hope but a truth that remembers our sovereignty as unceded, as ongoing, and embodied. Accepting the truth of the limitations of this place offers us far more promise than hope ever has.

It is in the retirement of hope that we are forced to return to, and remember, who we are and where we are from. We are forced to reckon with our own form of turning up, our own notions of survival, our own terms of reference. For it is in that moment of realisation, after all is said and done and sacrificed, that there is nothing you can do to change who the fuck they are, that we must remember who the fuck we are. Coming to the reality that justice is only reserved for those they've deemed human is not to accept our own inhumanity – but instead to realise theirs, and the futility of expecting anything better from them. It means telling the truth about Black power and white violence rather than Black dysfunction and supposed white benevolence, which tragically we have been force-fed so long that too many of us have come to believe that our lives are dependent upon it.

It always amazes me the excitement some Blackfullas have in having good white people as neighbours, friends or employers/employees, as though their being decent to Black people is a benevolence that needs applause. That some colonisers may not need to be as invested as others in directly perpetuating colonial violence offers me no more hope in this place – it just reminds me how little energy they need expend in holding us down.

From a childlike race and not fully human, to a dying race of a people who aren't fully or really Aboriginal: no place they reserve for us holds promise, materially or ideologically. All the talk of gap closing and problem-solving, and the conflation of sovereignty with service-delivery arrangements configured around us as social problems, is informed by the same racialised ideologies that enable them to forget that where they came from is not the land in which we became human. But colonial settlerism demands of us a forgetting – forgetting that we were ever Indigenous in the first place. Why, then, would we want to invest our hope in such a goal?

The strategy for living in this place is found not in their hopes or mountain tops, but in the ugly truths told in the songs of the marginalised. Du Bois claims that hope was breathed throughout all of the sorrow songs of the slave, a hope he defines as 'a faith in the ultimate justice of things'.[22] While pondering whether such hope is justified, Du Bois speaks of hope as a 'faith in life, sometimes a faith in death, sometimes assurance of boundless justice in some fair world beyond'.[23]

I'd argue, however, that there is a distinct difference between hope and faith. Faith is the assurance of knowing, a belief in things. Hope, on the other hand, is less certain; something that may or may not arrive at an unknown time. Hope is futile for Blackfullas and contradictory to articulations of Black sovereignty, which rely upon a certain truth of knowing who we are, in spite of what they say about us. To have a form of faith only in a world beyond sings clearly to the uselessness of hope in Black living as articulated by Black folk from elsewhere, who speak of life in a land in which they did not become human.

To accept that it's the nihilism that makes life worth living is to accept the meaninglessness of the place they have reserved for us. Retiring hope is to relinquish having hope in colonial institutions predicated upon our non-existence. If we take nihilism as our starting point, maybe we will be more strategic with the sacrifices we are prepared to make, and demand more from those we once invested our hopes in. Maybe we might even stem the tide of Black deaths on the frontline.

fuck hope

In making a case for retiring hope as a strategy, I am often met with, 'Okay, so I get that it really is that bad, but what is the solution?' When I suggest that the solution is Black living, I frequently encounter a blank stare. It is as though Black living is not enough; but what more worthy task could there be, what more 'hopeful' solution are they seeking?

Aunty Lilla Watson reminds us of the need to imagine a future as long as the past that is behind us. As the oldest living culture in the world, survival has been central to our existence and must continue to be. If anyone can theorise, teach and tell of survival and the strategies necessary for living, it would be us; it would be here, right now.

When I speak of survival I don't mean in the desperation sense, but the enduring 60,000 years 'still here' sense. The 'always was, always will be' form of survival; the persisting, insisting, enduring, resisting and thriving kind of survival. And central to our survival right now is knowing that there isn't any mountain top, or bran nue dae, given the simple fact that they aren't leaving.

It is a survival that strategises a way of living around a coloniser existence predicated upon our non-existence. It is living a life that requires us to get up each day and step out onto a playing field where the rules are predefined yet always changing to ensure that our demise and despair will always be deemed predestined and natural.

It really is easy to take up a fight you know you will win. But to live in a game that you know you'll never win, no matter how clever you know yourself to be, you best believe in the importance of strategising survival, and rearranging those damn corner posts. It is a survival that demands we re-arm ourselves not with new knowledge, but the old knowledges grounded in our ways of knowing, being and doing. Indigenous survival in a colonial-settler state is a turning up even when we know we are meant to lose; it is a standing still kind of turning up, much like the conflict resolution processes within our communities, knowing this conflict will never be fully resolved or reconciled. We are trapped in a daily existence where the odds are stacked against us, but it is in our being, in our turning up, that our sovereignty, through our insistence, is embodied and enacted, regardless of what they say and do. Our bodies hold power – a power not dependent upon the myths of white hope. Our living is not tied to winning, for it is in our being.

We have so much to teach this place about what it is to live fully. Sadly, in the space of so-called Indigenous studies, there is a preoccupation with a lost and past way of life, rather than an Indigenous presence, either current or future. Even the health sciences, which are meant to be concerned with our health, are still fixated upon Black death, Black disease, Black dysfunction and Black despair. The colonisers hold out no hope for us as a people who have survived because their lives are dependent upon our supposed hopelessness. So the act of living demands of us a refusal, a refusal to accept their account of things and a refusal to let them rob us anymore of our joy, our life and our land. Of course there are too many days where we all grow weary, but it is in those moments we must remember 'sometimes it's the nihilism that makes life worth living'.

It wasn't so long ago that I believed in blue-sky moments as an alternative to race transcendentalism. Du Bois speaks of these moments, of 'beating them at a running race, or beating them in an exam or beating their stringy heads'.[24] As someone who had done all of those things and enjoyed those blue-sky moments, I really thought that those blue-sky moment wins would give me enough oxygen for living. But I remember going to Aunty Lilla and proudly telling her of my pursuit of those blue skies as a way to satisfy my stubborn curiosity for what justice might feel like. She advised me that we were never to see justice, in that we will never have returned to us what they have taken. She then questioned me as to why I needed to win. Why was my being in the world predicated upon wresting something from the coloniser protagonist, knowing that it wouldn't restore us whole? She reminded me that our being on our terms is winning, of the everyday kind.

When we operate on our terms, we already know more than them. We don't need their wins to sustain our lives. It really is a peculiar sensation to know one's body as a battleground, as a strategy and a solution, but such is the power of an embodied Indigenous sovereignty.

fuck hope

For those of you still clinging to the life raft of hope, I understand that right now you feel you need it. But just know you can only

211

hold on to it for a minute, like that breath you must hold when you're swimming underwater. Remember, though, you need to come up to breathe eventually – there is only so long that we can hold our breath, hold on to hope. Because hope is just a matter of holding on – it does not give oxygen to your lungs, it just stops the water from entering them, and as a long-term strategy it is bound to kill you. To emerge from that water, to take a breath, is to be sovereign. And both are found in the living.

These aren't metaphors. I am talking about the ability to breathe in this place. To live. To carve out an existence. It is not an illusory space – it is real, and only made real through a critical Black realisation, of our past and our future. It is we who imagine that future, not them. And it is up to us to imagine a future that is grounded in truth, the truth of our sovereignty as ongoing and, as such, an insistence that must be made every day; a persistence that doesn't always centre coloniser protagonists, but a living that is grappling with our own selves on our terms.

In retiring hope, we are freed from those other lies we have learnt to live with, or felt we needed in order to live here. And what is left is the truth of our lives and our land. And the truth is, there is a most beautiful power in the unwavering self-belief of Blackfullas, grounded not in the individual but in the place from which we came. When Blackfullas realise our own power – we are the most powerful.

When you stop fighting to climb that mountain top, you come to see the power of the work done at the margins, and you discover the beauty of the marginalised. I love living on the border of Brisbane, whether to the south or to the west – where ugly foundries and industrial estates reside – because of the people who are found there and the sense of community that is created or rather maintained among all of that concrete. Even if it's out of necessity, to need Black community is far more freeing than reliance upon white validation – a validation that can be retracted over one false move. There is a security, strength and richness in the most impoverished Black communities – because it's in the Black community that sovereignty is embodied every day, where appeals to whiteness aren't applauded but fights for Black causes are.

I remember conversations I've had with a good friend, Franny Lomas, over the years about raising our children in Inala. I remember her once taking her son to play football for a neighbouring club, instead of our local club, West Inala, which is composed predominantly of Blackfullas and was fairly under-resourced. She spoke of returning him to West Inala, because 'it's just not the same singing out the name of other places'. I never forgot that conversation, the dispossessing act of pretending to barrack for another side, of another place. Since then Franny has been responsible for building that club into what it is today; no longer having any children of her own on the field, she still turns up every weekend to make sure Blackfullas can represent their own community.

You see, realising the hopelessness in other things enables us to realise our own beauty and strength and the importance of building up things that are exclusively for us. Black nihilism is not a place of hopelessness, but a place of joy, peace and justice – because we have deemed ourselves worthy of those things, because we choose to pursue them having conceptualised those things on our terms.

fuck hope

Black nihilism, in all of its supposed hopelessness, means an existence framed on our terms, and not on our non-existence. It means freeing up that wasted time to attend to things that matter to us first, and refusing to be of service to the coloniser and their things. Black nihilism in all of its supposed ugliness is also the place in which I have found joy, a joy more rewarding than those occasional blue-sky moments. There is much possibility in this place for a sovereignty that is embodied and enacted by us and there is a joy in theorising sovereignty as survival in the everyday, as opposed to clinging to white hope and Black hopelessness.

I remember sitting in my first race discrimination pre-tribunal conciliation by myself with three senior white men: lawyer, manager and commissioner. It was the first time I tested Queensland's race discrimination laws and I had no legal representation and no idea what I was doing. I had no idea what I had got myself into, though I knew I was right to hold them accountable, but in the moment of that face-to-face meeting my body was feeling something physically. My heart was racing and all of the unexpected nerves had channelled themselves through my left leg, which was tapping up and down under the table. In that moment I remembered my body as sovereign, as powerful and not alone in that room. I told myself, 'be sovereign', over and over again until I believed it. I stopped that leg from moving uncontrollably, and I held my head high like I was told to.

And as I'm familiar with the usual game of bluff the commissioner plays in these processes, where the goal is to keep the case from going to a full hearing, I was unsurprised that they started on me first. He went in, intimidating me about the cost, the legal expertise that I lacked, the burden of proof, while looking smugly at the two white male perpetrators beside me. Unwavering I insisted I was up for it, and made my case.

Within minutes I was asked to vacate the room so he could persuade the other party, but in my absence so as not to humiliate them – a privilege not afforded me, of course. But in under thirty minutes I walked out with what I wanted for the family who I had represented, precisely because in that moment I remembered I was sovereign. I walked out of the building on my own, feeling good that I had secured a small win, and it was here that I first felt the emancipatory possibility of not giving a fuck.

Many times since I've had to sit in rooms with the odds stacked against me on my own with white people who occupy powerful positions. In those meetings I now take up the disingenuous offer of water, not because I am thirsty but because I want them to see my unshaking hand every time I place the cup to my lips.

I remember entering a conciliation process with my

countryman Dr Derek Chong as the silent support person. Like a boss, he rearranged the room we were to sit in, to ensure that we held the power in that space. In that meeting there wasn't a win in terms of an outcome, but there was a win in our being, in our turning up. Afterwards we enjoyed a nice lunch and discussed our respective plans for the weekend as though it had been just another day, because it had.

The meeting could have been traumatic and indeed one of the independent conciliator's concluding remarks, where she claimed that my perpetrators 'respected me', reminded me of the solidarity of white people in race discrimination processes in whatever role they play. But because I knew who I was, I knew that comment was reflective of her inability to do her job properly and not a reflection of the merit of my case. That this time I took mob with me reminded me of the importance of a sovereignty that does not reside in the lone Black body, and of the importance of the Black collective in holding that frontline for each other.

The next time I took another brother, Kevin Yow Yeh, as my support in the process. When he arrived he asked me questions, questions that he knew would require me to articulate the things I needed to tell myself before entering the battleground. In that meeting, the perpetrators kept referring to me as 'Mizz Bond' in a snarky manner. I interjected, advising them that my name was either Dr Bond or Mrs Bond, and that they were free to pick the appropriate title. They repeatedly Mizz'ed me, and I repeatedly reminded them who the fuck I was. When mob stand with us, the assertion of who we are becomes all the more possible and all the more pleasurable. Man, did we laugh after that meeting!

I have been in countless meetings with colonisers who hold positions of power where they perform a care or interest or helpfulness, but fail to actually offer anything. Rather than allow them to impose a sense of disorienting and dispossessing hope or helplessness upon my body, I find joy in dealing with the truth of things and acting accordingly – it really confuses them.

I had seen Blackfullas orchestrate these turns before, of confusing white people, and it is a sight. I think of Uncle Coco Wharton and the mob suddenly bursting into a sprint on Brisbane streets during G20 protests and the confused police running after them. It is a remembering of our power in what they want us to believe are our most powerless moments. It is a remembering that we are in control, and that we belong here in ways that they never can. And because this place holds and protects us, we have nothing to fear, and sure as hell nothing to lose. But that's the greatest limitation of hope for Blackfullas, that what sits underneath it is fear, which is a most fucking useless emotion as the foundation of one's living.

It is freedom, not fear, that must form the parameters for our existence. Let me return to Edward Said and his representations of the exiled intellectual, and the possibilities of an unmitigated Blackness. Being the exiled intellectual, he writes:

means being liberated from the usual career, in which 'doing well' and following in time-honoured footsteps are the main milestones. Exile means that you are always going to be marginal, and that what you do as an intellectual has to be made up because you cannot follow a prescribed path. If you can experience that fate not as deprivation and as something to be bewailed, but as a sort of freedom, a process of discovery in which you do things according to your own pattern, as various interests seize your attention, and as the particular goal you set yourself dictates; that is a unique pleasure.

The exilic intellectual does not respond to the logic of the conventional but to the audacity of daring, and to representing change, to moving on, not standing still.[25]

fuck hope. be sovereign.

a final word ... on joy

Dean's Commendation for
Outstanding PhD 2007

Dr Chelsea Bond

"When you're black, they look at you harder": narrating aboriginality within public health

University of Queensland theses are examined by world leaders in the field. The assessors of this thesis commended its substantial contribution to the field of research. Dean's Commendations are awarded to fewer than ten percent of PhD or MPhil graduates.

Professor Christa Critchley
Dean
UQ Graduate School

14 July 2008

THE UNIVERSITY OF QUEENSLAND
AUSTRALIA

I have a duty to speak the truth as I see it and share not just
my triumphs, not just the things that felt good, but the pain, the
intense, often unmitigated pain. It is important to share how I
know survival is survival and not just a walk through the rain.

Audre Lorde[1]

When doing work on the margins you may find 'yourself'
all by yourself. It's a lonely place some days. In these places
you can find yourself abandoned: abandoned by the institution
you laboured excessively for, and the officers within it who
once were friends or at least colleagues; the union who was
supposed to fight for you, or at least protect you, you thought;
not to mention the others who don't want to be tarnished by
association with the troublemaking you've apparently brought
upon yourself. At times you may have to insist on being by
yourself to prevent bystanders being caught in the crossfire.
Whether by choice or not, the loneliness of that place can play
tricks on your mind, in such a way that you start to doubt
yourself. 'Maybe there's something wrong with me ... maybe
I should keep quiet and go along with things. I mean, I am
the common denominator after all. Why can't I just shut my
mouth?'

chelsea watego

Some days, it's a scary place to be, to feel as though you are in disagreement, in a battle of some sort, so frequently that you feel like the perpetual protagonist in your own story, on your own land. It's not a whole lot of fun being cast as a caricature of a troublemaker in ways that negate the legitimate transformative work that you do in your unwavering stance.

Sometimes it's hard to force a smile or make idle chitchat with those who in their mediocrity frequently discredit you but never have the courage to run straight at you with their critique. Some days we can only see the depth of our wounds, which are so deep that they sometimes prevent us from remembering the kind of nihilism that makes life worth living or fighting for. Some days giving up seems like a logical and rational conclusion of things. Death, for the race destined to die, is always imminent.

Sometimes we may feel betrayed by those we thought were standing on the frontline with us who have quietly faded into the shadows when we glance to our left. In fact, that happens a lot. But some days we cannot see those beside us, not because they aren't there; it's just in the midst of the battle they aren't in our line of sight because we are consumed by the sheer volume of the enemies ahead of us.

Some days we are so focused on minimising the assaults upon our bodies that we can't feel the force of those behind us. Some days we can get overwhelmed by the numbers of those against us, particularly when they include those who we thought were supposed to be with us. But we have to remember that this isn't a numbers game. Survival for Blackfullas in the colony, of the

224

life worth living kind, is a matter of strategy – because it indeed is 'not just a walk in the rain'.[2]

One of the things that most offends me in all of this, in the midst of the fights, in the moments shortly after having been brutalised, is the advice I would routinely be offered by those who seemed to be sitting on the sidelines of it all, and sometimes even by those who occupied positions of power to do something about it all. That advice, always offered with the best of intentions, was a most condescending instruction to 'take care of yourself'.

I hate being told to take care of myself; as if I am not already. 'Take care of yourself' typically implies that you've forgotten to care, that in fighting back you are incapable of knowing yourself, or your worth, or that your feelings of worthlessness are a result of your inability to care, and not a legitimate response to the violence you've experienced.

As if I don't know that I have 'to be the strongest weapon in the most gallant struggle of our lives'.[3] And this idea that you can care yourself out of oppressive structures is the ultimate form of gaslighting. I mean, after all, the directive to 'take care of yourself' is an instruction for you, and not a call upon the social world to be accountable to you. As if my current predicament is a result of me not having taken care. The directive to take care of oneself in the midst of defending oneself is a gesture of care without actually doing a thing. Yet it is my predicament, that battle or conflict that is itself evidence of me having taken care of myself, in deeming myself worthy of fighting for, even when no-one else does.

I've never been a fan of self-care, at least the white women Pinterest version of self-care where bubble baths, yoga, hikes and massages are all claimed as 'acts of political warfare'. Those words, taken up by white women the world over, actually came from the journal of a Black lesbian mother, warrior, poet, the great Audre Lorde. At the time of writing that quote she wasn't alone in the woods with her thoughts and nature; she was travelling the globe fighting injustice anywhere and everywhere while also working out how best to fight the cancer that was killing her. Yes, at the same time.

You see, self-care has been used to rationalise retreats to private quiet places, to places of comfort and indulgence, away from and out of the struggle, all the while being framed as though it is some kind of emancipatory strategy. But self-care really is some self-serving shit. I've seen self-care used too often by those sitting on mountain tops lecturing those working tirelessly at the margins to quell their activism rather than care for their wellbeing. Because in all of their self-care they have found too much comfort in the world they inhabit, so much so that they forget there is a fight being had every day and everywhere in this place, which is being undertaken by those they are telling to take care of themselves.

But this isn't a matter of caring for oneself or not. This is a matter of returning to a notion of selfhood that doesn't place itself above all else, but a notion of selfhood that is relational. When I speak of the Black self as a Blackfulla, I don't speak of it as a body divorced from other Black peoples or places, even when they come from other Indigenous nations. Self-care in a most radical Blackfulla sense is to love the Black body — all of them, not just our own. I'm not talking about solidarity, but a relationality that extends to care, that too is lived, lived in the acts of Blackfullas.

Black self-care is Alison Whittaker turning up to coroner's courts, it's Amy McQuire insisting on Kevin Henry's innocence, it's Ruby Wharton with a megaphone, it's Barkaa telling her tittas not to hang their head in a noose, it's Murrawah Johnson fighting the biggest coalmine in the world, it's Lorna Munro fighting gentrification, it's Fiona Foley memorialising massacre sites, it's Gwenda Stanley's voice echoing down city streets, it's Tarneen Onus-Williams burning it down, it's CJay's Vines, it's *Wild Black Women* everywhere all the time — those Black women who refuse to accept that comfort that silence promises in the course of 'self-care' and 'self-preservation'. It is a Black self-care that finds itself in solidarity with Blackness above all else, which includes, while not centring, your damn self.

Wemba Wemba and Gundijtmara woman Paola Balla declares, 'To be sovereign is in fact to act with love and resistance simultaneously',[4] because there isn't a choice between care of the self and fighting on frontlines for Black women in this place. To do so demands a disconnect, another form of dispossession from the Black bodies we birthed or were birthed from. To enact an existence that is always love and resistance demands of us a deliberate and conscious decision to find joy — not away from the fight, but in the fucking fight. I mean if I'm always going to be in it, I may as well have fun doing it. That is what it means to care for oneself too.

bell hooks in conversation with Jackie Huggins spoke of Black love 'as a political force that can mediate some of the tensions that arise'.[5] It is Black love that spurs me to fight but that also brings me joy in the midst of it all. I have had so much joy in battles, but particularly through the joy that it brings other Blackfullas. I remember doing a debate at La Trobe University in 2019 on the topic 'Has racism in Australia entered the political mainstream?' and what I loved was not so much giving it to my opponents but watching the joy that it gave Blackfullas.[6] Similarly, going on national television and giving it to the colonisers doesn't give me joy in itself, rather it is the mob's reaction to the spectacle of it all that nourishes me.

I love the joy that fighting for Blackfullas brings to Blackfullas. I still remember early on when Angelina Hurley and I were doing *Wild Black Women* and one morning having just finished the show and racing to my day job as an academic, Uncle Vern Hopkins rang me up. He rarely calls me, so I knew I was in trouble, and sure enough his boisterous deep voice rang down the phone. Turns out our show had made him pull his car off the road and listen and laugh along, which had made him late. I remember the joy I felt after that phone call, even in having made him late.

I remember the joy of sitting at our favourite Vietnamese restaurant in Inala when sister Yula Monkland regaled us with a retelling of the story of how she quit a job that she had laboured over for eight years while never being permitted to advance. She quit in the most spectacularly Black fashion of all, unleashing all of the insults she could muster at all of those

228

in management positions who had at some point placed their heel upon her neck. She had done things that many at that table wouldn't dare, having been told that the selection panel would not waste their time in giving her the opportunity of an interview for a promotion. The rage that came from being told that any time devoted to her would be wasted brought us all immense joy. She re-enacted every line with a 'and then I said' as we roared with laughter. There is so much joy to be found in turning over the tables that we've been denied a seat at, and it is the place where Blackfullas really live life in its fullest sense.

I remember the feeling of freedom that joy brought to the table in that moment. And I remembered that our breathing was still laboured, but only because of the knee slapping, hand clapping, screams and snorts of laughter. And, yeah, sis doesn't have a job, but she went in the next day and got her reference, and walked out with her dignity intact and her sovereignty unceded.

There is so much joy to be found in these moments of radical Black self-care and love and insistence, and it doesn't come in the winning of the blue-sky kind in their courts or on their terms, but in the embodied sovereignty of Blackfullas as it is exercised every day in the colony. As Audre Lorde said:

I work, I love, I rest, I see and learn. And I report. These are my givens. Not sureties, but a firm belief that whether or not living them with joy prolongs my life, it certainly enables me to pursue the objectives of that life with a deeper and more effective clarity.[7]

endnotes

introduction

1   Ah Kee, V 2009, 'borninthisskin', art installation.

2   Jones, BT 2019, 'Rough Seas Ahead: Why the government's James Cook infatuation may further divide the nation', *The Conversation*, 23 January, <https://theconversation.com/rough-seas-ahead-why-the-governments-james-cook-infatuation-may-further-divide-the-nation-110275>.

3   SBS News 2019, 'Shorten takes aim at Scott Morrison's "Captain Cook fetish"', *SBS*, 31 January, <https://www.sbs.com.au/news/shorten-takes-aim-at-scott-morrison-s-captain-cook-fetish>.

4   Cook, J, Beaglehole, JC & Skelton, RA 1955, 'The Journals of Captain James Cook on His Voyages of Discovery', retrieved 17 February 2021, <http://nla.gov.au/nla.obj-588382830>.

5   Koori-Rep, MC Mooks & Graydz 2019, 'Resuscitation', song, *The Game Changer*, Blkfulla Entertainment.

6   Kunoth-Monks, R 2014, 'I Am Not the Problem', speech, *Q&A*, ABC TV, 9 June, <https://www.youtube.com/watch?v=birnA3_tm5E>.

7   Mukandi, B & Bond, C 2019, '"Good in the Hood" or "Burn It Down"? Reconciling Black presence in the academy', *Journal of Intercultural Studies*, vol. 40, no. 2, pp. 254–68.

chapter 1

1   Fanon, F 1959, *A Dying Colonialism*, from the 1967 edition, Grove Press, New York, p. 130.

2   Ah Kee, V 2007, Dark + Disturbing, 'Dark + Disturbing is a curatorial project that explores Aboriginal sensibilities around knowledge, identity, and protest. It interrogates power structures and provides a platform for Aboriginal voice. "Dark + Disturbing"

references the place the "aborigine" holds in this country. The "aborigine" is either rendered invisible, as in terra nullius, or is made negative and pathologised as a problem or a curse.', <https://www.darkanddisturbing.com.au/about/>.

3   Du Bois, WEB 1903, *The Souls of Black Folk*, from the 2018 edition, *The Souls of Black Folk by WEB Du Bois with a Critical Introduction by Patricia Hinchey*, Myers Education Press, Gorham.

4   *ibid.*, p. 9.

5   Ah Kee, V 2007, Dark + Disturbing, 'Aboriginal people are part of a system of control that requires us, in order to survive/exist, to take on the tropes of the wider society. In the interest of survival persistence and existence, as Aboriginal people we are not willing participants.',   <https://www.darkanddisturbing.com.au/shop/notawillingparticipant/>.

6   Du Bois, WEB, *The Souls of Black Folk*, p. 8.

7   Ah Khee, V 2007, Dark + Disturbing, 'He says, When we were kids, my dad used to say you had to be "Aboriginal all the time". What he meant was, he'd worked with people who were performing Aboriginality while they were at work, and then forget they were Aboriginal when worked stopped. He said "if you work for Aboriginal people you should be Aboriginal all the time".', <https://www.darkanddisturbing.com.au/shop/aboriginal-all-the-time/>.

8   Bond, C 2007, '"When you're black, they look at you harder": Narrating Aboriginality within public health', unpublished PhD thesis.

9   Chauvel, C 1955, *Jedda*, Charles Chauvel Productions Ltd, <https://www.youtube.com/watch?v=GKR5H0DWjEU>.

10   Aboriginal Reconciliation Branch, The Department of the Prime Minister and Cabinet 1996, 'A New Beginning: Community attitudes towards Aboriginal reconciliation', study no. 9413, p. 14, <https://parlinfo.aph.gov.au/parlInfo/download/publications/tabledpapers/HSTP08999_1996-98/upload_pdf/8999_1996-98.pdf;fileType=application%2Fpdf#search=%22publications/tabledpapers/HSTP08999_1996-98%22>.

11   Fanon, F 1963, *The Wretched of the Earth*, Grove Press, New York, p. 236.

12 Mabo v Queensland (No. 2), 1992, 175 CLR 1. This decision by the High Court of Australia held for the first time in Australian law that native title rights continued to exist.

13 Ah Khee, V 2019, Dark + Disturbing, 'In a country like Australia, everyone is racist because everything relates to race. As long as there is an oppressed peoples, particularly its native people, then absolutely everything is "because racism"', <https://www.darkanddisturbing.com.au/shop/because-racism/>.

14 Putnam, W 2012, '"Please don't feed the natives": Human zoos, colonial desire, and bodies on display', FLS, The Environment, vol. XXXIX, pp. 58.

15 Moreton-Robinson, A 2000, Talkin' Up to the White Woman: Aboriginal women and feminism, University of Queensland Press, St Lucia, p. 242.

16 Bond, C, Brough, M & Cox, L 2014, 'Blood in Our Hearts or Blood on Our Hands? The viscosity, vitality and validity of Aboriginal "blood talk"', International Journal of Critical Indigenous Studies, vol. 7, no. 2, pp. 1–14.

17 Bell, R 2002, 'Bell's Theorem: Aboriginal art – it's a white thing!', <http://www.kooriweb.org/foley/great/art/bell.html>.

18 Morrison, T 1987, Beloved, Penguin, p. 190.

19 Cope, M 2013, 'Megan Cope is a member of the proppaNOW Collective. I'm Not Afraid of the Dark reflects White Australia's fear of blackness.', <https://www.darkanddisturbing.com.au/shop/im-not-afraid-of-the-dark/>.

20 Allam, L 2018, '"In 1788 it was nothing but bush": Tony Abbott on Indigenous Australia', The Guardian, 29 August, <https://www.theguardian.com/australia-news/2018/aug/29/in-1788-it-was-nothing-but-bush-tony-abbott-on-indigenous-australia>.

21 Lorde, A 1984, The Master's Tools Will Never Dismantle the Master's House, from the 2018 edition, Penguin Classics.

22 Bond, C, '"When you're black, they look at you harder"'.

23 Bond, C & Singh, D 2020, 'More than a Refresh Required for Closing the Gap of Indigenous Health Inequality', Medical Journal of Australia, vol. 212, no. 5, pp. 198–9.

24 Moreton-Robinson, A 2016, Critical Indigenous Studies: Engagements in first world locations, University of Arizona Press.

25 Du Bois, WEB, *The Souls of Black Folk*, p. 8.

26 Mukandi, B & Bond, C 2019, '"Good in the Hood" or "Burn It Down"? Reconciling Black presence in the academy', *Journal of Intercultural Studies*, vol. 40, no. 2, pp. 254–68.

27 Bond, C, Whop, L, Brough, M, Mukandi, B, Macoun, A, Newhouse, G, Drummond, A, McQuire, A, Stajic, J & Kajlich, H 2021, 'Black to the Future: Making the case for Indigenist health humanities', special issue of the *International Journal of Environmental Research and Public Health: The health and wellbeing of Indigenous and tribal peoples around the globe*, forthcoming.

28 Bond, C, Singh, D & Tyson, S, 'Black Bodies and Bioethics: Debunking mythologies of benevolence and beneficence in contemporary Indigenous health research in colonial Australia', *Journal of Bioethical Inquiry*, vol. 18, no. 1, pp. 83–92.

29 *ibid.*

30 Keogh, L 2011, 'Sandstone Dreams', *Crossroads*, vol. 5, no. 2, pp. 7–17, <http://www.uq.edu.au/crossroads/Archives/Vol%205/Issue%202%202011/Vol5Iss211%20-%205.Keogh%20(p.7-17).pdf>.

31 Deloria Jr, V 1969, *Custer Died for Your Sins: An Indian manifesto*, from the 1988 edition, University of Oklahoma Press, Norman, pp. 256–7, <https://mvlindsey.files.wordpress.com/2015/08/custer-died-for-your-sins-deloria-jr-1987.pdf>.

32 Du Bois, WEB, *The Souls of Black Folk*, p. 2.

33 Fanon, F, *The Wretched of the Earth*, pp. 236–48.

34 Ah Khee, V 2013, Dark + Disturbing, 'Deadly is a popular term among Aboriginal people. It can mean great, good, fast, strong, knowledgeable.', <https://www.darkanddisturbing.com.au/shop/i-see-deadly-people/>.

35 Inala Wangarra is an Indigenous community development organisation that provides a range of programs that strengthen community participation in business, economic and social enterprise development. See Mukandi, B, Singh, D, Brady, K, Willis, J, Sinha, T, Askew, D & Bond, C 2019, '"So we tell them": Articulating strong Black masculinities in an urban Indigenous community', *AlterNative: An international journal of Indigenous peoples*, vol. 15, no. 3, pp. 253–60.

36 Bond, C 2016, 'Why I struggle with the idea of Struggle Street

filming in my suburb', *The Conversation*, 19 May, <https://theconversation.com/why-i-struggle-with-the-idea-of-struggle-street-filming-in-my-suburb-59678>.

37 Ah Khee, V 2010, Dark + Disturbing, 'still here was originally created by Vernon Ah Kee in 2010 in response to continued questions about Aboriginal sovereignty. Despite their terra nullius, their attempts to assimilate, their racism, Aboriginal people are still here', <https://www.darkanddisturbing.com.au/shop/still-here/>.

38 Moreton-Robinson, A 2015, *The White Possessive: Property, power, and Indigenous sovereignty*, University of Minnesota Press, Minneapolis, p. 17.

chapter 2

1 Goldberg, DT 2009, *The Threat of Race: Reflections on racial neoliberalism*, Wiley-Blackwell, Oxford, p. 4.

2 Drummond, A 2020, 'Embodied Indigenous Knowledges Protecting and Privileging Indigenous Peoples' Ways of Knowing, Being and Doing in Undergraduate Nursing Education', *The Australian Journal of Indigenous Education*, vol. 49, no. 2, pp. 127–34, 128.

3 Kirk, A 2006, 'Abbott suggests "new paternalism" solution to Indigenous disadvantage', *AM*, ABC Radio, 21 June, <https://www.abc.net.au/am/content/2006/s1667987.htm>.

4 Leane, J 2016, 'Other Peoples' Stories', *Overland*, 225 summer, <https://overland.org.au/previous-issues/issue-225/feature-jeanine-leane/>.

5 'Closing the gap' is the policy approach by which the Australian government has committed to address health inequities by setting various ongoing targets and timeframes by which these disparities will be 'overcome'. Despite recent policy attempts to refresh and revise the strategy, with over a decade of failed policy targets, there has yet to be an interrogation of the assumptions that underpin this policy approach. See Bond, C & Singh, D 2020, 'More than a Refresh Required for Closing the Gap of Indigenous Health Inequality', *Medical Journal of Australia*, vol. 212, no. 5, pp. 198–9.

6 Whittaker, A 2019, 'Not My Problem: On *The Colonial Fantasy*', *Sydney Review of Books*, <https://sydneyreviewofbooks.com/

review/maddison-colonial-fantasy/>.

7 There is an extractive violence in research that can only see Black bodies as untethered fragments. See Bond, C, Singh, D & Tyson, S 2021, 'Black Bodies and Bioethics: Debunking mythologies of benevolence and beneficence in contemporary Indigenous health research in colonial Australia', *Journal of Bioethical Inquiry*, vol. 18, no. 1, pp. 83–92.

8 Chauvel, C 1955, *Jedda*, Charles Chauvel Productions Ltd, <https://www.youtube.com/watch?v=GKR5H0DWjEU>.

9 McQuire, A 2019, 'Black and White Witness', *Meanjin Quarterly*, winter, <https://meanjin.com.au/essays/black-and-white-witness/>.

10 Goldberg, DT, *The Threat of Race*, p. 4.

11 Bond, C 2019, 'Talkin' Down to the Black Woman', *Australian Feminist Law Journal*, vol. 45, no. 2, <https://www.tandfonline.com/doi/full/10.1080/13200968.2020.1837536>.

12 Fanon, F 1963, *The Wretched of the Earth*, Grove Press, New York, p. 236.

13 Hassal, AJ 2002. 'Introduction', *To the Islands*, University of Queensland Press, St Lucia, p. x.

14 *ibid.*

15 Behrendt, L 2016, *Finding Eliza: Power and colonial storytelling*, University of Queensland Press, St Lucia, p. 5.

16 Stow, R 2002, 'Preface to the Revised Edition', *To the Islands*, University of Queensland Press, St, Lucia, p. xiii.

17 Whittaker, A 2019, 'Not My Problem: On *The Colonial Fantasy*'.

18 *ibid.*

19 See; Huggins, J 1998, *Sister Girl: The writings of Aboriginal activist and historian Jackie Huggins*, University of Queensland Press; Holt, A 2001, *Forcibly Removed*, Magabala Books; Hegarty, R 2003, *Is That You Ruthie?*, University of Queensland Press; Williams, L 2015, *Not Just Black and White*, University of Queensland Press.

20 Leane, J, 'Other Peoples' Stories'.

21 Whittaker, A, 'Not My Problem: On *The Colonial Fantasy*'.

22 *ibid.*

23 Leane, J 2014, 'On Cannibals; Spur of the moment 2014', *Hecate*, vol. 39, no. 1, p. 171.

24 Langton, M 1994, 'Aboriginal Art and Film: The politics of

representation', *Race & Class*, vol. 35, no. 4, pp. 89–106.

25 Wright, A 2016, 'What Happens When You Tell Somebody Else's Story? A history of Aboriginal disempowerment', *Meanjin Quarterly*, summer, pp. 58–76, <https://meanjin.com.au/essays/what-happens-when-you-tell-somebody-elses-story/>.

26 Huggins, J, *Sister Girl*, p. 25.

27 Zhou, D 2019, 'Lionel Shriver returns to Australia and doubles down on "fascistic" identity politics', *The Guardian*, 2 September, <https://www.theguardian.com/books/2019/sep/02/lionel-shriver-returns-to-australia-and-doubles-down-on-fascistic-identity-politics>.

28 Flood, A 2020, '"Real censorship": Roxane Gay responds to *American Dirt* death threat row', *The Guardian*, 14 February, <https://www.theguardian.com/books/2020/feb/13/roxane-gay-death-threats-american-dirt>.

29 Fanon, F 1963, *The Wretched of the Earth*, pp. 236–48.

30 Deloria Jr, V 1969, *Custer Died for Your Sins: An Indian manifesto*, from the 1988 edition, University of Oklahoma Press, Norman, pp. 251–2, <https://mvlindsey.files.wordpress.com/2015/08/custer-died-for-your-sins-deloria-jr-1987.pdf>.

31 Aunty Mary Graham is a Kombu-merri person through her father's heritage and a Wakka Wakka clan through her mother's heritage. She has worked across government, community organisations and higher education for over thirty years and was appointed Associate Adjunct Professor at the University of Queensland and awarded an Honorary Doctorate from the Queensland University of Technology for lifetime commitments to scholarship and community, <https://www.theblackcard.com.au/dr-mary-graham/>.

32 Bond, C 2016, 'The White Man's Burden: Bill Leak and telling "the truth" about Aboriginal lives', *The Conversation*, 5 August, <https://theconversation.com/the-white-mans-burden-bill-leak-and-telling-the-truth-about-aboriginal-lives-63524>.

33 Archibald-Binge, E 2017, 'Indigenous academic shocked to see son labelled "trouble maker" in Education Queensland image', *NITV News*, 7 September, <https://www.sbs.com.au/nitv/article/2017/09/06/indigenous-academic-shocked-see-son-labelled-trouble-maker-education-queensland>.

34 McCarty, C 2014, 'Get out and teach remote', *Queensland Country Life*, 14 December, <https://www.queenslandcountrylife.com.au/story/3367790/get-out-and-teach-remote/>.
35 Behrendt, L, *Finding Eliza*, p. 5.
36 McCarty, C, 'Get out and teach remote'.
37 Peer review feedback received via email correspondence, 12 September 2018.
38 Moreton, R [@IndigenousX], 1 December 2019, *Who are sovereign storytellers? All Indigenous peoples since time immemorial. We are storytellers & great at it. In fact, we've kept a whole country humming for thousands of years through the power of our storytelling*, Twitter, <https://twitter.com/IndigenousX/status/1200947150449807360?s=20>.
39 McQuire, A 2019, 'Black and White Witness'.
40 McLennan, C 2016, *Saltwater*, University of Queensland Press, St Lucia.
41 Mason, G 2016, 'Third sly grog sentence handed down by Far North Queensland magistrate reduced on appeal', *The Cairns Post*, 15 August, <https://www.cairnspost.com.au/news/crime-court/third-sly-grog-sentence-handed-down-by-far-north-queensland-magistrate-reduced-on-appeal/news-story/296e141b4526735472eb60fdbabf0729>.
42 Bond, C, 'Talkin' Down to the Black Woman'.
43 Sender's name omitted at request of *Australian Feminist Law Journal* editors, 'Re: Your article in AFLJ, and handling legal matters', personal correspondence, 2 February 2020.
44 Bond, C, 'Talkin' Down to the Black Woman'.

chapter 3

1 Langton, M 1994, 'Aboriginal Art and Film: The politics of representation', *Race & Class*, vol. 35, no. 4, p. 95.
2 Leane, J 2016, 'Other Peoples' Stories', *Overland*, 225 summer, <https://overland.org.au/previous-issues/issue-225/feature-jeanine-leane/>.
3 *ibid.*
4 Wright, A 2016, 'What Happens When You Tell Somebody Else's Story?', *Meanjin Quarterly*, summer, <https://meanjin.com.au/essays/what-happens-when-you-tell-somebody-elses-story/>.

5   Wright, A, 'What Happens When You Tell Somebody Else's Story?'; Leane, J, 'Other Peoples' Stories'.

6   Adichie, CN 2009, 'The Danger of a Single Story', *TEDGlobal*, 0:10:12.

7   *ibid.*, 0:12:45.

8   *ibid.*, 0:13:45.

9   Eliza Fraser was a Scottish woman and wife of Captain James Fraser, who along with the ship's crew became shipwrecked off Fraser Island in 1836. Taken in by the Butchulla people for several weeks and later 'rescued' by an escaped convict, she retold her story of supposed ill-treatment at the hands of the Butchulla. Variations of her story have been reproduced and reimagined in cinema, fiction and paintings.

10 Behrendt, L 2016, *Finding Eliza: Power and colonial storytelling*, University of Queensland Press, St Lucia, p. 5.

11 *ibid.*, p. 192.

12 Ellen was the name of the lead character in Patrick White's novel *A Fringe of Leaves*, which was based on Eliza Fraser's experiences.

13 Behrendt, L, *Finding Eliza*, p. 5.

14 *ibid.*, p. 25.

15 *ibid.*, p. 5.

16 *ibid.*, p. 7.

17 *ibid.*, p. 44.

18 *ibid.*, p. 7.

19 *ibid.*, p. 37.

20 *ibid.*, p. 9.

21 *ibid.*, p. 23.

22 *ibid.*, p. 23.

23 McLennan, C Law Week Justice Journeys: Magistrate Cathy McLennan, <https://www.justice.qld.gov.au/corporate/events-seminars/law-week/justice-journeys-old/staff-profiles/magistrate-cathy-mclennan>.

24 *ibid.*

25 *ibid.*

26 McLennan, C 2016, *Saltwater*, University of Queensland Press, St Lucia.

27 *ibid.*

28   Shaw, P 2009, *Seven Seasons in Aurukun: My unforgettable time at a remote Aboriginal school*, Allen & Unwin, Crows Nest.

29   Vass, G 2011, 'Seven Seasons in Aurukun: My unforgettable time at a remote Aboriginal school', *Discourse: Studies in the cultural politics of education*, vol. 32, no. 1, pp. 161–4.

30   McLennan, C, *Saltwater*, p. vi.

31   Fernbach, N & Tapiolas, P 2016, 'Queensland magistrate's book, *Saltwater*, raises questions around Indigenous youth crime', *ABC News*, 17 August, <http://www.abc.net.au/news/2016-08-17/queensland-magistrates-book-raises-issues-around-youth-crime/7751674>.

32   McLennan, C, *Saltwater*, p. 311.

33   'Palm Island riots: Federal Court finds police acted with "impunity" in racial discrimination lawsuit', *ABC News* (online), 5 December 2016, <http://www.abc.net.au/news/2016-12-05/palm-island-riots-federal-court-upholds-discrimination-suit/8093182>. The Federal Court awarded Palm Island resident Lex Wotton $220,000 in damages resulting from a successful action against the Queensland Government and Queensland Police Commissioner in a racial discrimination action relating to the 2004 Palm Island riots and death of Mulrunji.

34   McLennan, C, *Saltwater*, p. 103. McLennan's account indicates that most Aboriginal characters refer to her as 'Caffey'. This seems to be despite their ability to pronounce almost all other 'th' sounds appropriately, as suggested by an interaction recounted by McLennan in which an Aboriginal woman makes an introduction to McLennan: 'Caffey, this my sister Elizabeth'.

35   *ibid.*, p. 13.

36   *ibid.*, p. 8.

37   *ibid.*, p. 8.

38   *ibid.*, pp. 12–13.

39   *ibid.*, p. 15.

40   *ibid.*, p. 15.

41   *ibid.*, p. 15.

42   *ibid.*, p. 18.

43   *ibid.*, p. 19.

44   *ibid.*, p. 80.

45 *ibid.*, p. 34.
46 *ibid.*, p. 53.
47 *ibid.*, p. 53.
48 *ibid.*, p. 54.
49 *ibid.*, p. 53.
50 *ibid.*, p. 267.
51 *ibid.*, p. 299.
52 *ibid.*, p. 299.
53 *ibid.*, pp. 54, 83.
54 *ibid.*, pp. 22, 78, 141, 198, 217.
55 *ibid.*, pp. 120, 166.
56 *ibid.*, p. 94.
57 *ibid.*, p. 220.
58 *ibid.*, p. 120.
59 *ibid.*, p. 166.
60 *ibid.*, p. 225.
61 *ibid.*, pp. 19, 23, 31.
62 Leane, J 2014, 'White's Tribe: Patrick White's representation of the Australian Aborigine in *A Fringe of Leaves*', in Cynthia vanden Driesen and Bill Ashcroft (eds), *Patrick White Centenary: The legacy of a prodigal son*, Cambridge Scholars Publishing, pp. 263–5.
63 McLennan, C, *Saltwater*, p. 21.
64 Leane, J, 'White's Tribe'.
65 McLennan, C, *Saltwater*, pp. 3, 294.
66 *ibid.*, pp. 15, 19, 95, 115, 282.
67 *ibid.*, pp. 53, 129, 181, 184, 264, 268, 294, 298.
68 *ibid.*, p. 141.
69 *ibid.*, p. 141.
70 *ibid.*, p. 166.
71 *ibid.*, pp. 120, 217.
72 *ibid.*, pp. 94, 212.
73 *ibid.*, pp. 41, 199, 268, 287.
74 *ibid.*, pp. 93, 271.
75 *ibid.*, pp. 53, 180.
76 *ibid.*, pp. 65, 181, 195, 202, 209, 255, 257, 294, 296, 299, 301.
77 *ibid.*, p. 64.
78 *ibid.*, p. 19.

79 *ibid.*, pp. 67, 135, 168.
80 *ibid.*, p. 115.
81 *ibid.*, p. 221.
82 *ibid.*, pp. 224, 267.
83 *ibid.*, p. 32.
84 *ibid.*, pp. 32, 187.
85 *ibid.*, p. 227.
86 *ibid.*, p. 197.
87 *ibid.*, p. 291.
88 *ibid.*, p. 21.
89 *ibid.*, pp. 22, 149.
90 *ibid.*, pp. 24, 219.
91 *ibid.*, p. 45.
92 *ibid.*, pp. 35, 182, 197.
93 *ibid.*, pp. 42, 292.
94 *ibid.*, pp. 83, 142, 189, 206, 271.
95 *ibid.*, p. 76.
96 *ibid.*, p. 84.
97 *ibid.*, p. 294.
98 *ibid.*, pp. 294, 298.
99 *ibid.*, pp. 88, 176.
100 *ibid.*, pp. 120, 121, 142.
101 *ibid.*, pp. 120, 121.
102 *ibid.*, pp. 15, 18, 47, 137.
103 *ibid.*, p. 300.
104 *ibid.*, p. 189.
105 *ibid.*, p. 21.
106 *ibid.*, p. 47.
107 *ibid.*, p. 48.
108 *ibid.*, p. 45.
109 *ibid.*, pp. 53, 55, 81, 138, 142, 154, 183, 184, 198, 221, 224, 227, 267, 285, 291.
110 *ibid.*, pp. 120, 202.
111 *ibid.*, p. 125.
112 *ibid.*, pp. 137, 173, 198, 217, 287.
113 *ibid.*, p. 212.
114 *ibid.*, pp. 200, 209.

115 *ibid.*, p. 217.
116 *ibid.*, p. 250.
117 *ibid.*, p. 184.
118 *ibid.*, p. 294.
119 *ibid.*, pp. 94, 138, 246, 271.
120 *ibid.*, p. 94.
121 *ibid.*, p. 21.
122 *ibid.*, pp. 64, 168, 189, 199, 219.
123 *ibid.*, p. 120.
124 *ibid.*, p. 153.
125 *ibid.*, pp. 162, 225.
126 *ibid.*, p. 187.
127 *ibid.*, pp. 120, 199.
128 *ibid.*, p. 259.
129 *ibid.*, p. 69.
130 *ibid.*, p. 281.
131 *ibid.*, p. 277.
132 *ibid.*, p. 94.
133 *ibid.*, p. 270.
134 *ibid.*, p. 140.
135 *ibid.*, p. 22.
136 *ibid.*, p. 22.
137 *ibid.*, p. 42.
138 *ibid.*, p. 33.
139 *ibid.*, p. 48.
140 *ibid.*, p. 39.
141 *ibid.*, p. 43.
142 *ibid.*, p. 108.
143 *ibid.*, p. 128.
144 *ibid.*, p. 137.
145 *ibid.*, pp. 61, 147.
146 *ibid.*, p. 151.
147 *ibid.*, pp. 22, 287.
148 *ibid.*, pp. 22, 23.
149 Angelo Rich Robinson observes that the 'enslaved Southern "mammy" did not appear as a stereotype until the 1830s' and served as a dominant white narrative for adult Black women in

the South who 'served white families as wet nurses, nannies, and generally oversaw childcare and housekeeping'. Robinson, AR 2011, '"Mammy Ain't Nobody Name": The subject of Mammy revisited in Shirley Anne Williams's Dessa Rose', *Southern Quarterly*, vol. 49, no. 1, p. 51.

150 McLennan, C, *Saltwater*, pp. 32, 110, 123.

151 *ibid.*, p. 32.

152 *ibid.*, p. 206.

153 *ibid.*, p. 56.

154 *ibid.*, pp. 32, 37, 56, 160.

155 *ibid.*, pp. 32, 45, 206.

156 *ibid.*, pp. 45, 56.

157 *ibid.*, p. 56.

158 *ibid.*, p. 208.

159 *ibid.*, pp. 45, 161.

160 *ibid.*, pp. 45, 48, 197.

161 *ibid.*, p. 45.

162 *ibid.*, p. 48.

163 *ibid.*, pp. 45, 48, 197, 208, 305.

164 *ibid.*, p. 45.

165 *ibid.*, p. 206.

166 *ibid.*, pp. 206, 207. McLennan describes Aunty Arriet, field officer and her colleague, getting stuck 'underneath the desk ... on all-fours, back-end poking out' as she 'grunts [and] moans' to 'triumphantly' retrieve a muesli bar for McLennan.

167 *ibid.*, p. 307.

168 Behrendt, L, *Finding Eliza*, p. 202, emphasis added.

169 McLennan, C, *Saltwater*, p. 310.

170 Behrendt, L, *Finding Eliza*, p. 193.

171 *ibid.*, p. 184.

172 *ibid.*, p. 186.

173 Nowra, L 2007, *Bad Dreaming: Aboriginal men's violence against women and children*, Pluto Press, North Melbourne; McLennan, C, *Saltwater*, p. 53, in which McLennan describes a 16-year-old Aboriginal boy as looking as though 'he'd make a good baddie in a film'.

174 Huggins, J 1998, *Sister Girl: The writings of Aboriginal activist and*

historian Jackie Huggins, University of Queensland Press, St Lucia, p. 2.

175 Wright, A, 'What Happens When You Tell Somebody Else's Story?'.

176 Huggins, J, *Sister Girl*, p. 6.

177 Langton, M 1993, 'Well, I Heard It on the Radio and I Saw It on the Television: An essay for the Australian Film Commission on the politics and aesthetics of filmmaking by and about Aboriginal people and things', Australian Film Commission, Sydney.

178 Moreton-Robinson, A 2013, 'Towards an Australian Indigenous Women's Standpoint Theory', *Australian Feminist Studies*, vol. 28, no. 78, pp. 331, 340.

179 Leane, J 2016. 'On Cannibals', States of Poetry ACT – Series One, *Australian Book Review*, <https://www.australianbookreview.com.au/poetry/states-of-poetry/states-of-poetry-act>.

chapter 4

1 Ahmed, S 2017, *Living a Feminist Life*, Duke University Press, Durham, pp. 9–10.

2 Bell, D 1992, 'Racial Realism', *Connecticut Law Review*, vol. 24, no. 2, p. 363.

3 Pryor, BM 2018, *Wrong Kind of Black*, four-part web series, ABC iview.

4 Mukandi, B & Bond, C 2019, '"Good in the Hood" or "Burn It Down"? Reconciling Black presence in the academy', *Journal of Intercultural Studies,* vol. 40, no. 2, pp. 254–68.

5 Morrison, T 1975, 'A Humanist View', *Oregon Public Speakers Collection: Black Studies Center public dialogue. Pt. 2*, Portland State University, Oregon, <https://pdxscholar.library.pdx.edu/orspeakers/90/>.

6 Du Bois, WEB 1903, *The Souls of Black Folk*, from the 1994 edition, Dover, New York, p. 2.

7 Fanon, F 1959, *A Dying Colonialism*, from the 1970 edition, trans. Haakon Chevalier, Pelican, Ringwood, p. 65.

8 Huggins, J 1998, *Sister Girl: The writings of Aboriginal activist and historian Jackie Huggins*, University of Queensland Press, St Lucia, p. 25.

9   Smith, S & Clarke, M 2017, 'Meet the Bonds: What does it mean to be "Aboriginal middle class"?', *Foreign Correspondent*, ABC, 28 June, <https://www.youtube.com/watch?v=MN7pMgKOafU>.

10 Hall, S 1983, 'Teaching Race', *Early Child Development and Care*, vol. 10, no. 4, pp. 259–74.

11 Smith, S & Clarke, M, 'Meet the Bonds'.

12 Singh, D 2020, 'Racial Complaint and Sovereign Divergence: The case of Australia's first Indigenous ophthalmologist', *The Australian Journal of Indigenous Education*, vol. 49, no. 2, pp. 145–8.

13 Mansell quoted in Moreton-Robinson, A 2007, 'Introduction: Sovereign subjects', in Moreton-Robinson, A (ed.), *Indigenous Sovereignty Matters: Sovereign subjects*, Allen & Unwin, Crows Nest, p. 2.

14 Quote from Cathy Freeman in the film *Freeman*, 2020, directed by Laurence Billiet, Matchbox Pictures & General Strike.

15 Langton, M 1988, 'Medicine Square', in Keen, I (ed.), *Being Black: Aboriginal cultures in 'settled' Australia*, Aboriginal Studies Press, Canberra, pp. 201–25.

16 Carmichael, S 1966, 'What We Want', *The New York Review of Books*, from a reprint by the Santa Clara Valley Friends of the Student Nonviolent Coordinating Committee.

17 Thorpe, N 2018, '#IStandWithTarneen: People stand in solidarity with young Aboriginal activist under fire for controversial comments', *NITV/SBS*, 31 January, <https://www.sbs.com.au/nitv/nitv-news/article/2018/01/30/istandwithtarneen-people-stand-solidarity-young-aboriginal-activist-under-fire>; Rosalie Kunoth-Monks appears on *Q&A* responding to Peter Coleman's critique of John Pilger's documentary film *Utopia* and that assimilation is not the answer, *ABC News*, 5 November 2014, <https://www.abc.net.au/news/2014-11-05/rosalie-qanda/5869432?nw=0>.

18 Singh, D & Sweet, M 2018, 'RANZCO urged to apologise to first Indigenous ophthalmologist – and more news from #MovingBeyondTheFrontline', *Croakey*, 8 November, <https://croakey.org/ranzco-urged-to-apologise-to-first-indigenous-ophthalmologist-and-more-news-from-movingbeyondthefrontline/>.

19 Singh, D, 'Racial Complaint and Sovereign Divergence'.

19 Singh, D, 'Racial Complaint and Sovereign Divergence'.
20 Wildie, T 2019, 'Photographer who captured iconic Nicky Winmar racism image reflects ahead of statue unveiling', *ABC News*, 5 July, <https://www.abc.net.au/news/2019-07-05/story-behind-the-iconic-nicky-winmar-photo/11282028>.
21 Huggins, J, *Sister Girl*, p. 6.
22 Watego, C 2021 'Always Bet on Black (Power): The fight against race in the colony'. *Meanjin Quarterly*, spring.

chapter 5

1 Deloria, PJ 1998, *Playing Indian*, Yale University Press, New Haven, pp. 90–1.
2 Personal communication from Associate Professor Lisa Whop, who asks, 'but where are your cousins?'
3 Bond, C, Brough, M & Cox, L 2014, 'Blood in Our Hearts or Blood on Our Hands? The viscosity, vitality and validity of Aboriginal "blood talk"', *International Journal of Critical Indigenous Studies*, vol. 7, no. 2, pp. 1–14.
4 Bond, C 2007, '"When you're black, they look at you harder": Narrating Aboriginality within public health', unpublished PhD thesis.
5 The subheadings throughout this chapter use lyrics from Archie Roach's 'Took the Children Away', reproduced with permission from Mushroom Music.
6 Ramsden, I 2002, 'Cultural Safety and Nursing Education in Aotearoa and Te Waipounamu', PhD thesis, <https://croakey.org/wp-content/uploads/2017/08/RAMSDEN-I-Cultural-Safety_Full.pdf>.
7 Richards, J 2008, *The Secret War*, University of Queensland Press, St Lucia.
8 Wolfe, P 2006, 'Settler Colonialism and the Elimination of the Native', *Journal of Genocide Research*, vol. 8, no. 4, p. 388, <https://www.tandfonline.com/doi/full/10.1080/14623520601056240>.
9 Tuck, E & Yang, WK 2012, 'Decolonization Is Not a Metaphor', *Decolonization: Indigeneity, education & society*, vol. 1, no. 1, p. 10.
10 Moreton-Robinson, A 2015, 'I Still Call Australia Home: Indigenous belonging and place in a postcolonizing society',

The White Possessive: Property, power, and Indigenous sovereignty, University of Minnesota Press, Minneapolis.

11 Lyrics reproduced with permission from Mushroom Music.

12 Langton, M 1993, 'Well, I heard it on the radio and I saw it on the television: An essay for the Australian Film Commission on the politics and aesthetics of filmmaking by and about Aboriginal people and things', Australian Film Commission, Sydney.

chapter 6

1   Beatty, P 2016 *The Sellout*, Oneworld Publications, London.

2   Said, E 1996, *Representations of the Intellectual: The 1993 Reith lectures*, 1st Vintage ed., Vintage Books, New York.

3   Du Bois, WEB 1903, *The Souls of Black Folk*, from the 1994 edition, Dover, New York.

4   Watson, I 2015, *Aboriginal Peoples, Colonialism and International Law: Raw law (Indigenous peoples and the law)*, Routledge, New York, p. 4.

5   Beatty, P, *The Sellout*, p. 277.

6   Russell, A 2016, 'Author Paul Beatty on satire, *The Sellout* and the pain of writing', *The Wall Street Journal*, 27 October, <https://www.wsj.com/articles/author-paul-beatty-on-satire-the-sellout-and-the-pain-of-writing-1477586972>.

7   Davis, A 1971, 'Lectures on Liberation', Committee to Free Angela Davis, New York, p. 4.

8   Beatty, P, *The Sellout*, p. 275.

9   McQuire, A 2017, 'Amy McQuire on Token Recognition, and Sam Thaiday's Misogyny', 15 May, <https://newmatilda.com/2017/05/15/amy-mcquire-on-token-recognition-and-sam-thaidays-misogyny/>.

10 Beatty, P, *The Sellout*, p. 276.

11 Beatty, P, *The Sellout*, pp. 267–77.

12 *ibid.*, p. 277.

13 Mukandi, B & Bond, C 2019, '"Good in the Hood" or "Burn It Down"? Reconciling Black presence in the academy', *Journal of Intercultural Studies*, vol. 40, no. 2, pp. 254–68.

14 Goldberg, DT 2009, *The Threat of Race: Reflection on racial neoliberalism*, Wiley-Blackwell, Oxford, p. 339.

Chi. © Universal Music Publishing MGB Australia Pty. Ltd. All rights reserved. International copyright secured. Reprinted with permission.

16 Mukandi, B & Bond, C, '"Good in the Hood" or "Burn It Down"?', pp. 254–68.

17 Bond, C & Singh, D 2020, 'More than a Refresh Required for Closing the Gap of Indigenous Health Inequality', *Medical Journal of Australia*, vol. 212, no. 5, pp. 198–9.

18 Du Bois, WEB, *The Souls of Black Folk*, final chapter on slave songs.

19 Lyrics reproduced with permission from Kobie Dee.

20 Du Bois, WEB, *The Souls of Black Folk*, p. 191.

21 Noonuccal, O 1970, *My People*, 5th edition, 2020, John Wiley & Sons, Richmond.

22 Tuck, E & Yang, KW 2012, 'Decolonization Is Not a Metaphor', *Decolonization: Indigeneity, education & society*, vol. 1, no. 1, p. 10.

23 Du Bois, WEB, *The Souls of Black Folk*, p. 197.

24 *ibid.*

25 *ibid.*, p. 2.

26 Said, E, *Representations of the Intellectual*, p. 64.

a final word ... on joy

1 Lorde, A & Tate, C 1983, *Black Women Writers at Work*, continuum, p. 261.

2 *ibid.*

3 Lorde, A 1988, *A Burst of Light*, from the 2017 edition, *A Burst of Light: And other essays*, Dover, p. 133.

4 Balla, P 2016, 'Sovereignty: Inalienable and intimate'. In Balla, P & Delany, M (ed.), *Sovereignty*, Australian Centre for Contemporary Art, Melbourne, p. 15.

5 Huggins, J 1998, *Sister Girl: The writings of Aboriginal activist and historian Jackie Huggins*, University of Queensland Press, St Lucia, p. 65.

6 Pearson, L & Cromb, N 2019, 'Dr Chelsea Bond delivers a masterclass in Indigenous excellence', *IndigenousX*, <https://indigenousx.com.au/dr-chelsea-bond-delivers-a-masterclass-in-indigenous-excellence/>.

7 Lorde, A, *A Burst of Light*, p. 100.

note on cover artwork

about the artwork

Cover photograph is from Michael Cook's 'Broken Dreams' series.

A journey, through the eyes of a young Aboriginal woman reflecting upon the first European settlers in Australia; these are her broken dreams.

Where have these strange people come from? What are the huge vessels they travel on and those particular skins they wear?

Her dreams conjure up visions of their stories; she imagines herself in these strange clothes and living with these material possessions. Her musings are curious rather than fearful – do they feel the same way she does? As her journey progresses, so does her realisation that their culture is not her culture. As time passes, she sees the impact these new settlers are having on her people.

Dreams broken, hopes replaced with despair, she begins to shed her newly clothed skin and returns to her roots to find freedom – the connection back to her land.

about the artist

Michael Cook is an Australian art photographer who worked commercially in Australia and overseas for twenty-five years before he began to make art photography in 2009, driven by an increasingly urgent desire to explore issues of identity. He is of mixed ancestry – some of which is Indigenous – and works from an Australian base. His photographic series are unique in their approach, evocatively recreating incidents that emerge from colonial history. His images unite the historical with the imaginary, the political with the personal.

the songs that brought joy
while writing this book

'All That You Have Is Your Soul', Tracy Chapman
'Attitude', Leikeli47
'Bam Bam', Sister Nancy
'Be Honest', Jorja Smith feat. Burna Boy
'Because I'm Me', The Avalanches
'Before I Let Go', Beyoncé
'Best Part', Daniel Caesar feat. H.E.R
'Better in Blak', Thelma Plum
'Black Child', Birdz feat. Mojo Juju
'Black Love', Papoose feat. Nathaniel
'Black Privilege', Miiesha
'Black Smoke', Emily Wurramara
'Brown Skin', Philly feat. Waari
'Burdens to Bear', Tiddas
'By Your Side', Tiddas
'Can I Kick It?', A Tribe Called Quest
'Can't Bring Me Down', Awreeoh
'Carry Me Home', Emily Wurramara
'Champion', Kanye West
'Coconut Oil', Lizzo

'Come Down Father', Beres Hammond

'Congratulations', Post Malone feat. Quavo

'Cool Enough', TeaMarrr

'Cruisin', Oetha

'Do Me Like That', Kalin White

'Don't Cry Dry Your Eyes', Fugees

'Ego', Beyoncé

'Everything', Impossible Odds feat. Georgia Corowa

'Everything I Am', Kanye West feat. DJ Premier

'F E M A L E', Sampa the Great

'Feel It Boy', Beenie Man

'Feelin' It', Jay-Z feat. Mecca

'Feeling Good', Nina Simone

'Floetic', Floetry

'Holy Ground', Davido feat. Nicki Minaj

'Infinity', Olamide feat. Omah Lay

'Let Me Know', Maleek Berry

'Like This', Kelly Rowland feat. Eve

'Lil Mama', Lo Village feat. Dirty Shafi

'A Lite', Buddy

'Loco (Remix)', Beele, Natti Natasha and Manuel Turizo, feat.
   Farruko

'Lose My Mind', L.A.X

'Lost Ones', Lauryn Hill

'Love in the Morning', Thutmose, Rema and R3HAB

'Manifesto', OverDoz

'May I', Flo Milli

'Me against the World', 2Pac feat. Dr Dre

'Miss Independent', Ne-Yo

'Mood', JessB

'Mood 4 Eva', Beyoncé, Jay-Z and Childish Gambino

'Mr La Di Da Di', Baker Boy

'Mulita', Leikeli47

'Murda', Seyi Shay feat. Patoranking and Shaydee

'Murder She Wrote', Chaka Demus and Pliers

'My Boo', Usher and Alicia Keys

'My Flag', Koori-Rep, MC Mooks and Graydz

'Nappy Heads', Fugees

'Nice for What', Drake

'No Fit Vex', Burna Boy

'Nwa Baby', Solidstar feat. 2Face

'OG Luv Kush pt 2', Kaiit

'Oh Heart', Tank and the Bangas

'On the Wire', Kev Carmody feat. Tiddas

'Ooh Na Na Na', Javada feat. Christopher Martin

'Options', Pitbull feat. Stephen Marley

'PAMI', DJ Tunez feat. Wizkid, Adekunle Gold and Omah Lay

'Party and Bullshit', The Notorious B.I.G

'Plastic', Moses Sumney

'Pon My Mind', Maleek Berry

'Pop a Bottle (Fill Me Up)', Jessica Mauboy

'Pretty Girl', Adekunle Gold and Patoranking

'Psycho', Post Malone feat. Ty Dolla $ign

'Rebirth of Slick (Cool like Dat)', Digable Planets

'Resuscitation', Koori-Rep, MC Mooks and Graydz

'ROXANNE', Arizona Zervas

'Sauce', Ella Mai

'Self Care', Miiesha

'She Don't Let Nobody', Chaka Demus and Pliers

'So Many Tears', 2Pac

'Still Sun', Obongjayar

'Supermodel', SZA

'Superstar', Lauryn Hill

'Sweet Thing', Rufus feat. Chaka Khan

'Therapy', Khalid

'Time Out', JessB feat. Abdul Kay

'Tip Toes', Saweetie feat. Quavo

'To Live and Die in LA', 2Pac

'To Zion', Lauryn Hill

'Too Late to Turn Back Now', Cornelius Brothers and Sister
    Rose

'Top Down', Kari Faux

'Touch It', KiDi

'Trampoline', Jidenna

'Trouble on Central', Buddy

'Waiting', Tiddas

'Win (Born 2 Win)', D12

'Wonderful', Burna Boy

'The World Is Yours', Nas

'You're the One', SWV

'22Clan', Barkaa and Mack Ridge